Good Housekeeping Cookery Club

*E*NTERTAINING

Maxine Clark

Bridgette & Gavin
lots of love
Emma-Lee & Brian
xxxxxx

EBURY PRESS
LONDON

First published 1994

1 3 5 7 9 10 8 6 4 2

First published in the United Kingdom in 1994 by Ebury Press
Random House, 20 Vauxhall Bridge Road, London SW1V 2SA

Random House Australia (Pty) Limited
20 Alfred Street, Milsons Point, Sydney,
New South Wales 2061, Australia

Random House New Zealand Limited
18 Poland Road, Glenfield,
Auckland 10, New Zealand

Random House South Africa (Pty) Limited
PO Box 337, Bergvlei, South Africa

Random House UK Limited Reg. No. 954009

A CIP catalogue record for this book is available from the British Library.

Managing Editor: JANET ILLSLEY
Design: SARA KIDD
Special Photography: GUS FILGATE
Food Stylist: MAXINE CLARK
Photographic Stylist: ROISIN NIELD
Techniques Photography: KARL ADAMSON
Food Techniques Stylist: ANNIE NICHOLS
Recipe Testing: EMMA-LEE GOW

ISBN 0 09 178543 X

Typeset in Gill Sans by Textype Typesetters, Cambridge
Colour Separations by Magnacraft, London
Printed and bound in Italy by New Interlitho Italia S.p.a., Milan

CONTENTS

COOKERY NOTES

- Both metric and imperial measures are given for the recipes. Follow either metric or imperial throughout as they are not interchangeable.
- All spoon measures are level unless otherwise stated. Sets of measuring spoons are available in metric and imperial for accurate measurement of small quantities.
- Ovens should be preheated to the specified temperature. Grills should also be preheated. The cooking times given in the recipes assume that this has been done.
- Where a stage is specified in brackets under freezing instructions, the dish should be frozen at the end of that stage.
- Size 2 eggs should be used except where otherwise specified.
- Use freshly ground black pepper unless otherwise specified.
- Use fresh rather than dried herbs unless dried herbs are suggested in the recipe.

INTRODUCTION

In the words of Brillat-Savarin, 'He or she who receives friends and pays no attention to the repast prepared for them is not fit to have friends . . . To invite a person to your house is to take charge of his/her happiness as long as he/she is beneath your roof'. Although sounding a little pompous, Brillat-Savarin had the right idea. Entertaining friends should be fun and relaxing, not only for your guests, but for yourself. All that is required is a little thought and careful planning.

The first golden rule is to avoid planning a meal that is too complicated. Do not tackle a recipe that is too involved or totally unfamiliar – as long as you are happy and confident with what you are providing, all will go well. A disaster could snowball and ruin the whole event. Have a small practice run on the family if you want to try something new and – if it works – why not freeze it for later and give the family something else!

When deciding on a menu, plan to keep it as well-balanced as possible. Think about the flavours, colours and textures – rich and light, sweet and savoury, crunchy and smooth – hot and cold. There are really no hard or fast rules, but don't have cream in all the courses, or fruit featuring in every dish, or

an all-brown menu. Above all, keep your choice simple.

Select produce in season wherever possible, when it is invariably at its peak for flavour and best value for money. Strawberries out of season, for example, are horrendously expensive and lacking in flavour! Glance at the seasonal menu suggestions opposite for some ideas. It is also worth finding out if anyone is a vegetarian or has any special dietary needs. So as not to cause any embarrassment, I often cook an entirely meatless meal if I know that there is going to be just one vegetarian – not as difficult as it sounds, and rarely does anybody notice! The menu opposite is suitable as long as – like mine – your vegetarian friend(s) are fish eaters!

It's a good idea to make a master shopping list, remembering to include paper napkins and candles if using. Decide which dishes are be made ahead and consider fridge and freezer space too. Invitations to a dinner party are best made over the phone about 10-12 days in advance. Always mention the type of occasion, whether formal or informal, time, date, address and if there are any special dress requirements – this avoids embarrassing situations! If you are sending written invitations, post these 2-3

weeks in advance to give people plenty of warning. Keep a list of invited guests and tick them off as they reply. Don't forget to include yourself in the numbers as I did once – write your name at the head of the list!

Check that table linen is laundered and ironed in advance and glasses and cutlery are clean. Clean the house 1-2 days before the event – not on the day or you will not be able to relax! Buy or order wine and drinks well in advance and avoid doing all the heavy shopping at once – it will seem much less of a chore!

We seem to live in a world that has little time for the simple things in life, cooking for friends being one of them. However you will find that the emphasis on the recipes in this book is speed of preparation and cooking, using the best and freshest of ingredients. Most of the dishes can be prepared up to a point and held, only needing a little last-minute finishing in the kitchen after you have joined your guests for a well-earned drink!

Keep the presentation simple and uncluttered which will complement the food, not hide it. You will notice that very few dishes in this book are elaborately garnished or decorated – the presentation of the food itself is usually enough.

MENU SUGGESTIONS

SPRING MENU
Warm Goat's Cheese Salad with Rocket Pesto

●

Lamb Cutlets with Minted Cucumber Salsa
OR
Pink Trout with Almond and Herb Purée
Creamy Mashed Potatoes with Chives
Selection of Green Vegetables

●

Rhubarb and Ginger Ice Cream with Ginger Biscuits

AUTUMN MENU
Vichyssoise with Lemon Grass

●

Pork Fillet with Garlic and Pepper Stuffing
Sweet Potato and Chestnut Cakes with Spring Onions
Steamed Broccoli

●

Coconut Bavarois with Tropical Fruit Sauce

COOK-AHEAD MENU
Aubergine, Mushroom and Coriander Pâté

●

Lamb Meatballs with Dill Sauce
Buttered Egg Noodles
OR
New Potatoes
Crunchy-topped Asparagus and Courgettes

●

Two-Chocolate Lace Pancakes
OR
Tiramisu Torte

SUMMER MENU
Chilled Tomato Soup with Avocado Cream

●

Char-grilled Spatchcock Poussins
OR
Smoked Salmon with Dill Tagliatelle
Boiled New Potatoes with Mint
Stir-Fried Summer Vegetables

●

Brown Sugar Meringues with Peaches
and Raspberry Sauce

WINTER MENU
Jerusalem Artichoke and Parmesan Soup

●

Beef Fillet with a Walnut Crust
Potato and Parsnip Galette
Grilled Chicory and Radicchio with
Orange and Pine Nuts

●

Walnut Tart with Caramel Ice Cream
OR
Coconut Bavarois with Tropical Fruit Sauce

NON-MEAT MENU
Herbed Ravioli with Wild Mushroom Filling

●

Roasted Monkfish with Mediterranean Vegetables
Bitter Green Salad with Citrus Dressing

●

Pistachio Praline Floating Islands

PREPARATION TECHNIQUES

For the fish and meat recipes in this book, you should be able to buy the particular cut ready-prepared from your local fishmonger, butcher or large supermarket. However, should you prefer to prepare the fish or meat yourself the following step-by-step guides will enable you to do so.

FILLETING AND SKINNING SOLE

To obtain four fillets from a whole fish proceed as follows:

1. Cut around the edge of the fish to outline the shape of the fillets with the tip of a sharp knife.

2. Cut through the skin and flesh just behind the gills in a 'V' shape. Cut a straight line through to the backbone along its length.

3. Keeping the knife flat and working against the bone, loosen the flesh away from the bones using short sharp strokes over the rib bones. Cut the sole fillet completely away.

4. Repeat with the other side to remove the second fillet. Turn the fish over and remove the other two fillets in the same way.

5. To skin each fillet, place the fillet skin side down, tail end towards you. Make a small cut at the tail to separate the flesh from the skin.

6. Dip the fingers of one hand in salt to help obtain a good grip and hold the skin at the tail end. Hold a filleting knife against the skin with the blade almost parallel to it, then push away from you in a sawing motion to release the flesh from the skin, holding the skin taught.

PREPARING MONKFISH

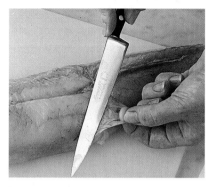

1. Using a filleting knife, trim off any remaining thin membrane from the outside of the fish.

2. Cut away any very dark meat from the monkfish.

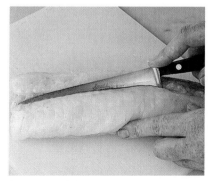

3. Slit the fish lengthways down the middle until you reach the bone. Turn the fish over and do the same on the other side.

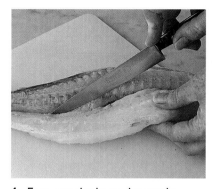

4. Ease out the bone, by gently scraping the flesh away with the knife. You will now have two fillets.

FILLETING A WHOLE SALMON

1. Using a filleting knife, cut through the skin from the head to the tail following the backbone.

2. Cut down to the backbone just behind the gill to release the thick end of the fillet.

3. Holding the knife flat and keeping the tip in contact with the bone, loosen the flesh away from head to tail using short sharp strokes. Hold the fillet away with the other hand.

4. Cut over the finer bones at the head end to free the fillet.

5. Turn fish over; remove second fillet in the same way. Cut into smaller fillets if required. Remove any remaining bones with tweezers.

PREPARING SCALLOPS

1. Scrub the scallop shells thoroughly under cold running water. Hold a scallop in the palm of your hand, rounded-side down, and take a medium-bladed knife in the other hand. Insert the knife between the shells and carefully slide it around the flat shell, severing the muscle. The shell should spring open.

2. Discard the empty top shell and loosen the scallop from the bottom shell by carefully sliding the knife under it.

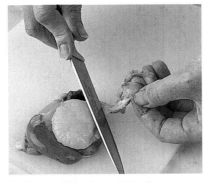

3. Trim off the beard-like fringe, being careful to avoid tearing the flesh. Separate the orange coral or roe from the white scallop if required. Rinse well.

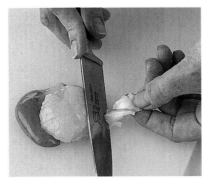

4. Cut away the little tough muscle at one side of the white meat and discard. Slice the scallop meat into rounds if necessary.

PREPARING A RACK OF LAMB OR BEST END OF NECK

The chine bone is normally removed by the butcher, if it isn't, ask him to do this for you – otherwise you will need a cleaver!

1. Lay the rack of lamb on a board, ribs uppermost, and cut out the yellow sinew from the base of the eye of the meat.

2. Cut out the small crescent of cartilage from one end of the rack. Pull off the thick outer layer of fat. (This may hold some meat that can be cooked along with the rack in the oven.)

SPATCHCOCKING A POUSSIN

This technique is applied to poussins and small game birds. The bird is split and flattened so that it can be grilled, barbecued or baked quickly and evenly.

3. Ribs down, score through the fat and meat to the bone about 7.5 cm (3 inches) from the end of the bones and cut off.

1. Using poultry shears, cut down one side of the backbone.

3. Open out the bird on a board and press down hard on the breast bone with the heel of your hand to break it and flatten the bird.

4. Cut out all the meat and fat from between the bones.

2. Cut down the other side of the backbone, then remove it. Snip the wishbone in half.

4. Thread two wooden or metal skewers crosswise through each bird to hold it in a flat position. Each skewer passes through a wing and out through the leg on the opposite side.

5. Scrape all fat and membrane from the bones.

CHILLED TOMATO SOUP WITH AVOCADO CREAM

A chilled, fresh soup of puréed ripe tomatoes and mint, topped with a smooth cream flavoured with avocado. This sophisticated soup needs no cooking and is best made with flavourful Italian plum tomatoes, which provide lots of colour too. Beef tomatoes would be a good substitute, but they must be very ripe.

SERVES 6

1.4 kg (3 lb) ripe red
    tomatoes
750 ml (1¼ pints) tomato
    juice
pinch of sugar
dash of Tabasco sauce
15 ml (1 tbsp) lemon juice
30 ml (2 tbsp) chopped fresh
    mint
salt and pepper
AVOCADO CREAM
1 large ripe avocado
10-15 ml (2-3 tsp) lemon
    juice
½ small onion
30 ml (2 tbsp) chopped fresh
    mint
90 ml (6 tbsp) soured cream
TO GARNISH
mint sprigs

PREPARATION TIME
20 minutes, plus chilling
COOKING TIME
Nil
FREEZING
Suitable: soup only (with the
diced tomato); stir well when
thawed. Do not freeze the
avocado cream.

145 CALS PER SERVING

1. Halve the tomatoes, then squeeze out the seeds into a bowl. Reserve 4 tomato halves and cut into fine dice, cover and refrigerate. Strain the tomato seeds through a small sieve to extract any juices; discard the seeds.

2. Place the remaining tomatoes in a blender or food processor with all the tomato juice, the sugar, Tabasco sauce, lemon juice, chopped mint and salt and pepper to taste. Liquidise or process until smooth, then pass through a sieve into a clean bowl. Taste and adjust the seasoning.

3. Cover and leave for at least 2 hours in the refrigerator to allow the flavours to develop and the soup to become thoroughly chilled.

4. Thirty minutes before serving, halve the avocado, remove the stone, then peel. Mash the avocado flesh in a bowl, using a fork, adding lemon juice to taste. Peel and finely grate the onion and mix into the avocado with the chopped mint and soured cream.

5. Stir the reserved diced tomato into the chilled soup. Ladle the soup into individual serving bowls and add a dollop of the avocado cream to each one. Garnish with mint to serve.

VARIATION

Substitute fresh basil for the mint. Dice the avocado and stir into the soup, leaving out the grated onion. Serve topped with spoonfuls of soured cream.

TECHNIQUE

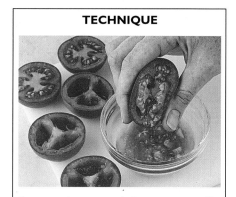

Squeeze the tomato halves over a small bowl to extract the seeds.

10

VICHYSSOISE WITH LEMON GRASS

This creamy, velvety soup is based on a popular classic – but with the added fragrance of oriental lemon grass. If possible, use fresh lemon grass, though you will find that dried is more readily available. To ensure a really smooth texture, it is important to liquidise and sieve the soup before serving, either hot or chilled.

SERVES 6

2 medium onions
450 g (1 lb) leeks (white part only)
175 g (6 oz) floury potatoes
1 lemon grass stalk (preferably fresh)
75 g (3 oz) butter
1.35 litres (2¼ pints) chicken stock
300 ml (½ pint) milk
150 ml (¼ pint) crème fraîche
salt and white pepper
TO SERVE
extra crème fraîche
chives, to garnish

PREPARATION TIME
15 minutes
COOKING TIME
30 minutes
FREEZING
Suitable: without the crème fraîche; add this when thoroughly thawed and reheated, whisking well

225 CALS PER SERVING

1. Peel and thinly slice the onions. Trim and slice the leeks. Peel and dice the potatoes. Bruise the lemon grass with the end of a rolling pin.

2. Melt the butter in a large saucepan and add the onions and leeks. Stir well, add 45 ml (3 tbsp) water, cover tightly and sweat over a gentle heat for 10 minutes until soft and golden.

3. Stir in the potatoes, lemon grass, chicken stock and milk. Bring to the boil, lower the heat, cover and simmer for 20 minutes until the potatoes are tender.

4. Discard the lemon grass. Allow the soup to cool slightly, then transfer to a blender or food processor and work until smooth. Pass through a sieve and return to the pan if serving hot.

5. Stir in the crème fraîche and seasoning to taste. Either cool and chill (in this case season really well) or reheat and pour into warmed soup bowls. Serve topped with a dollop of chilled crème fraîche and chives, to garnish.

NOTE: Fresh lemon grass is sold in the herb section of some supermarkets. It will freeze, but turns brown, which won't impair the flavour. Dried lemon grass is good too, as long as it isn't too old!

VARIATION

Replace the leeks with a bunch of spring onions, and add a bunch of trimmed and chopped watercress to the soup just before liquidising. The soup will be beautifully green, with a wonderful fresh taste.

TECHNIQUE

Bruise the lemon grass stalk by striking it firmly with the end of the rolling pin to release the flavour.

JERUSALEM ARTICHOKE AND PARMESAN SOUP

An unusual combination of mild Jerusalem artichokes with a hint of spice and the nutty taste of Parmesan cheese. The flavour of fresh Parmesan makes this soup really special. Don't be tempted to use the dry cheese sold in cartons – it bears no comparison to the real thing!

SERVES 6

450 g (1 lb) Jerusalem
   artichokes
2 shallots
50 g (2 oz) butter
5 ml (1 tsp) mild curry paste
900 ml (1½ pints) chicken or
   vegetable stock
150 ml (¼ pint) single
   cream (or milk for a less
   rich soup)
freshly grated nutmeg, to
   taste
pinch of cayenne pepper
60 ml (4 tbsp) freshly grated
   Parmesan cheese
salt and pepper
MELBA TOAST
3-4 slices day-old softgrain
   white bread
a little freshly grated
   Parmesan cheese, for
   sprinkling
1.25 ml (¼ tsp) paprika

PREPARATION TIME
15 minutes
COOKING TIME
25 minutes
FREEZING
Suitable

190 CALS PER SERVING

1. Scrub the Jerusalem artichokes thoroughly to remove any dirt. Pat dry, then slice thinly. Peel and dice the shallots.

2. Melt the butter in a large saucepan and add the shallots. Cook gently for 5 minutes until soft and golden. Stir in the curry paste and cook for 1 minute. Add the sliced artichokes and stock; stir well. Bring to the boil, cover and simmer for about 15 minutes or until the artichokes are tender.

3. Meanwhile, make the Melba toast. Preheat the oven to 180°C (350°F) Mark 4. Toast the bread lightly on both sides. Quickly cut off the crusts and split each slice in two. Scrape off any doughy bits, then sprinkle with Parmesan and paprika. Place on a baking sheet and bake in the oven for 10-15 minutes or until uniformly golden.

4. Add the cream, nutmeg and cayenne to the soup. Transfer to a blender or food processor and work until smooth, then pass through a sieve into a clean saucepan. Reheat the soup and stir in the Parmesan cheese. Taste and adjust the seasoning. Serve at once, with the hot Melba toast.

NOTE: If preferred the Melba toast can be prepared ahead, allowed to cool, then stored in an airtight tin. Warm through in the oven before serving.

VARIATION

Replace the Jerusalem artichokes with 1 large cauliflower. Cut away the leaves and core, and discard. Divide the cauliflower into florets. Add to the shallots with the stock and bring to the boil. Simmer for about 10 minutes or until very soft, then continue as in step 4.

TECHNIQUE

To make the Melba toast, carefully split each slice of toast horizontally in two. On baking these fine slices will curl.

AUBERGINE, MUSHROOM AND CORIANDER PÂTÉ

A luscious combination of smoky-flavoured creamy aubergine, dark savoury mushrooms and fresh tangy coriander. This rich vegetarian starter can be prepared as a chunky or smooth pâté as preferred. Served warm or cold, it is particularly good with toasted walnut bread.

SERVES 4-6

2 medium aubergines
2 shallots
225 g (8 oz) large flat
    mushrooms
45 ml (3 tbsp) olive oil
10-15 ml (2-3 tsp) crushed
    coriander seeds
45 ml (3 tbsp) dry white
    wine
60 ml (4 tbsp) chopped fresh
    coriander
salt and pepper
TO SERVE
coriander sprigs, to garnish
freshly toasted bread

PREPARATION TIME
20 minutes
COOKING TIME
1 hour
FREEZING
Suitable

140-95 CALS PER SERVING

1. Preheat the oven to 200°C (400°F) Mark 6. Place the whole aubergines on a baking sheet and bake for about 45 minutes or until soft and beginning to char.

2. Meanwhile, peel and finely chop the shallots. Wipe the mushrooms clean with a damp cloth, then chop finely.

3. Heat the oil in a medium saucepan and add the shallots and coriander seeds. Cook gently for 5 minutes until soft and golden. Stir in the mushrooms and wine and cook over a high heat for 10 minutes or until all the liquid has evaporated, stirring occasionally.

4. When the aubergines are cooked, split them open and scoop out the flesh. Chop the aubergine flesh roughly, then beat into the mushroom mixture. Stir in the chopped coriander and season well with salt and pepper. Either serve warm or allow to cool, then chill.

5. Serve the pâté garnished with spigs of coriander and accompanied by hot toasted bread.

VARIATION

Stir 125 g (4 oz) fromage frais into the cold pâté to give it a milder flavour and make it go further.

TECHNIQUE

Split each freshly baked aubergine lengthwise, then scoop out the soft flesh using a spoon.

WARM GOAT'S CHEESE SALAD WITH ROCKET PESTO

Thick slices of grilled goat's cheese are surrounded by sharp, peppery salad leaves dotted with walnuts, and topped with a tasty pesto made from rocket. A new twist on warm salads, the pesto has an affinity with creamy, tangy goat's cheese. The contrasts of warm and cold, peppery and creamy, make this salad very exciting.

SERVES 4

ROCKET PESTO
50 g (2 oz) rocket leaves
1 garlic clove
45 ml (3 tbsp) freshly grated
  Parmesan cheese
25 g (1 oz) shelled walnut
  halves
90 ml (6 tbsp) olive oil
pepper
SALAD
1 bunch watercress
50 g (2 oz) rocket leaves
40 g (1½ oz) shelled walnut
  halves
4 slices Bucheron chèvre
  (goat's cheese log with rind)
DRESSING
15 ml (1 tbsp) walnut oil
15 ml (1 tbsp) sunflower oil
5 ml (1 tsp) balsamic or
  sherry vinegar
salt and pepper

PREPARATION TIME
20 minutes
COOKING TIME
3-4 minutes
FREEZING
Not suitable

530 CALS PER SERVING

1. First make the rocket pesto. Place all the ingredients in a blender, food processor or herb mill and blend until smooth. Alternatively pound the ingredients together in a pestle and mortar. Cover with a thin layer of oil and set aside.

2. To prepare the salad, wash the watercress and rocket and trim if necessary. Store in a plastic bag in the refrigerator until needed.

3. Place all the dressing ingredients in a bowl and whisk well. Season with salt and pepper to taste.

4. Preheat the grill and briefly toast the walnuts until golden. Allow to cool. Place the goat's cheese slices on a foil-lined baking sheet and position as close to the grill as possible for 1-2 minutes, until browned.

5. Place a cheese slice on each serving plate and top with a spoonful of pesto. Toss the salad leaves with the dressing and arrange around the goat's cheese. Scatter over the grilled walnuts and serve immediately.

NOTE: The quantities for the rocket pesto make more than you require but it is impracticable to prepare a smaller amount. Any leftover pesto can be stored in a screw-topped jar in the refrigerator for up to 3 days.

VARIATIONS

Try using halved Crottins de Chavignol – small hard goat's cheeses instead of the Bucheron. Even a mound of soft fresh goat's cheese mixed with the pesto would be delicious. If you don't like goat's cheese, Cypriot halloumi cheese would make a good alternative.

TECHNIQUE

Blend the ingredients for the rocket pesto in a food processor, scraping down any bits that cling to the side of the bowl from time to time with a spatula.

Herbed Mushroom Ravioli

These pretty green herb-speckled ravioli are filled with a delicious mixture of wild mushrooms. Serve them simply topped with melted butter and freshly pared Parmesan cheese. A pasta machine gives excellent results, rolling the dough very finely – so that you may only need to use about two thirds of the quantity.

SERVES 6

PASTA
200 g (7 oz) type '00' pasta flour, or strong white bread flour
pinch of salt
2 (size 2) eggs
15 ml (1 tbsp) olive oil
45 ml (3 tbsp) mixed chopped fresh tarragon, marjoram and parsley

MUSHROOM FILLING
2 shallots
225 g (8 oz) mixed wild mushrooms *or* 175 g (6 oz) dark flat mushrooms, *plus* 40 g (1½ oz) dried porcini
25 g (1 oz) black olives
4 sun-dried tomatoes in oil
50 g (2 oz) butter
15 ml (1 tbsp) dry sherry
salt and pepper
freshly grated nutmeg
beaten egg, for brushing

TO SERVE
50 g (2 oz) butter, melted
few sautéed wild mushrooms
Parmesan cheese

PREPARATION TIME
55 minutes, plus resting
COOKING TIME
5 minutes
FREEZING
Suitable

550 CALS PER SERVING

1. To make the pasta, sift the flour and salt into a mound on a clean work surface and make a well in the centre. Beat the eggs and oil together, then pour into the well. Sprinkle in the herbs. Gradually mix the liquid into the flour using one hand, then bring the dough together.

2. On a clean surface, with clean hands, knead the pasta for 5-10 minutes until smooth and elastic. Wrap in cling film and allow to rest at room temperature for 30 minutes.

3. For the filling, peel and finely chop the shallots. Wipe or brush the fresh mushrooms clean, then chop finely. If using dried mushrooms, soak in hot water to cover for 10-15 minutes. Remove and chop finely. Strain the soaking liquid through a filter paper and reserve. Stone and finely chop the olives. Drain and finely chop the sun-dried tomatoes.

4. Melt the butter in a pan, add the shallots and cook for 5 minutes until soft and golden. Add all the mushrooms, olives and dried tomatoes; cook, stirring, over a high heat for 1-2 minutes. Add the sherry and reserved liquid; cook for 1 minute. Season well with salt, pepper and nutmeg. Transfer to a bowl; cool.

5. If using a pasta machine, roll manageable portions of dough into strips. If rolling out by hand, divide in half and roll into 2 sheets on a very lightly floured surface. Either way, roll out as thinly as possible and keep covered with a slightly damp tea towel.

6. Place 18 heaped spoonfuls of filling on one half of the pasta, spacing them at 4 cm (1½ inch) intervals. Brush the dough in between with beaten egg. Lift the other sheet(s) of pasta over the top. Press down firmly between the pockets of filling and cut into 7.5 cm (3 inch) squares. Transfer to a floured tea towel and leave to rest for 1 hour.

7. Bring a large pan of salted water to the boil, with a dash of oil added. Carefully add the ravioli, bring back to the boil, turn off the heat and cover with a tight-fitting lid. Leave for 5 minutes, then drain well. Serve immediately, on warmed plates, topped with the melted butter, sautéed mushrooms and shavings of Parmesan cheese.

TECHNIQUE

Lift the plain pasta over the ravioli filling, taking care to avoid tearing the dough.

SMOKED FISH TERRINE

A pretty white and pink-flecked fish mousse flavoured with a hint of orange. To complement the smoky flavour and cut through the saltiness, the mousse is best served with a sharp, crunchy salad. I like to serve it with an orange and sliced chicory salad, dressed with olive oil and orange juice.

SERVES 6

225 g (8 oz) undyed smoked
   white fish, such as
   haddock, cod, halibut
5 ml (1 tsp) finely grated
   orange rind
10 ml (2 tsp) orange juice
freshly ground white pepper
225 g (8 oz) smoked salmon
2 egg whites, chilled
150 ml (¼ pint) whipping
   cream, chilled
TO SERVE
dill sprigs, to garnish
orange and chicory salad
warm toasted bread

PREPARATION TIME
20 minutes
COOKING TIME
35-40 minutes
FREEZING
Not suitable

200 CALS PER SERVING

1. Cut up the white fish and remove any bones with tweezers. Place in a food processor or blender with the orange rind, orange juice and plenty of pepper. Blend until smooth. Cover the processor bowl and chill in the freezer for 10 minutes.

2. Meanwhile roughly chop the smoked salmon. Lightly oil or butter a 900 ml (1½ pint) terrine and line the base with greaseproof paper. Preheat the oven to 180°C (350°F) Mark 4.

3. Remove the processor bowl from the freezer and place on the machine again. With the machine running, add the egg whites through the feeder tube, then the cream; do not overwork or the mixture will curdle. Turn out into a bowl. Gently stir in the smoked salmon so the mixture is flecked with pink.

4. Carefully fill the terrine with the mixture, packing it down well to exclude trapped pockets of air, then level the surface. Cover the terrine with buttered greaseproof paper.

5. Stand the terrine in a roasting tin and pour in enough boiling water to come halfway up the side. Bake in the preheated oven for 35-40 minutes or until firm to the touch.

6. Run a thin-bladed knife around the terrine and unmould onto a warmed

platter. Cut into slices and arrange on individual plates. Garnish with dill and serve warm, with an orange and chicory salad, and warm toast.

VARIATION

Prepare individual timbales rather than a terrine. Divide the mixture between six 150 ml (¼ pint) individual metal moulds and bake as above in a bain-marie for 20 minutes or until firm to the touch.

TECHNIQUE

With the food processor running, pour in the cream in a steady stream through the feeder tube. Do not overwork the mixture, otherwise it will curdle.

SEARED SCALLOPS WITH ROASTED PLUM TOMATOES

This is a vibrant dish with the colours, the flavours and the simplicity I associate with Mediterranean food. Plum tomatoes are roasted to evaporate away some of their moisture, concentrating the flavour to recreate the sun-ripened sweetness of tomatoes from the Mediterranean. A simple leafy salad, some good bread and a glass of chilled wine are all I'd suggest to accompany.

SERVES 4

16 large fresh scallops,
    shelled (see page 8)
90 ml (6 tbsp) extra-virgin
    olive oil
2 garlic cloves
30 ml (2 tbsp) chopped fresh
    thyme or parsley
coarse sea salt and pepper
ROASTED TOMATOES
6 large plum tomatoes (or
    other flavourful
    tomatoes)
3 rosemary sprigs
juice of I small lemon

PREPARATION TIME
15 minutes
COOKING TIME
About 45 minutes
FREEZING
Not suitable

350 CALS PER SERVING

1. Preheat the oven to 180°C (350°F) Mark 4.

2. Rinse the scallops and pat dry with kitchen paper. Place in a bowl and spoon over 45 ml (3 tbsp) of the olive oil. Peel the garlic cloves and crush them to a paste on a chopping board with a little coarse sea salt. Add to the scallops with the chopped thyme or parsley. Season with pepper and mix well. Cover and refrigerate while preparing the tomatoes.

3. Cut the tomatoes lengthwise in half. Place them in one layer, cut side up, in a shallow baking tin. Add the rosemary and season liberally with sea salt. Drizzle over the remaining olive oil. Roast in the preheated oven for about 45 minutes until tender but still holding their shape.

4. About 10 minutes before the tomatoes are ready, preheat a large dry (not oiled) cast-iron griddle pan over a high heat for approximately 5 minutes. Lower the heat to medium.

5. To cook the scallops add them to the hot griddle pan in one layer. Allow to sizzle undisturbed for 1½ minutes, then turn each scallop and cook the other side for 1½ minutes.

6. To serve, lift the tomatoes from the baking tin and arrange on four warmed serving plates with the scallops and rosemary sprigs.

7. Tip the oil from the tomatoes into the griddle pan and add the lemon juice. Stir well and scrape up all the flavoursome sediment in the bottom of the pan as it sizzles. Trickle the juices over the scallops and roasted plum tomatoes and serve at once.

NOTE: A large griddle pan will take all of the scallops in a single layer, but if your pan is smaller you may need to cook them in two batches.

TECHNIQUE

Arrange the tomato halves, cut side up, in one layer in a shallow baking tin. Add the rosemary, sprinkle with sea salt and drizzle with olive oil before baking.

SMOKED SALMON WITH DILL TAGLIATELLE

This combination of delicate pink smoked salmon with a light butter sauce and ribbons of thinnest pale green pasta is quite stunning to look at and equally delicious! If preferred, flavour the pasta and sauce with other herbs, such as chives or parsley instead of dill.

SERVES 4

PASTA

300 g (10 oz) type '00' pasta
  flour or strong white
  bread flour
pinch of salt
3 eggs
15 ml (1 tbsp) olive oil
50 g (2 oz) fresh dill sprigs

BUTTER SAUCE

1 shallot
45 ml (3 tbsp) white wine
  vinegar
225 g (8 oz) unsalted butter,
  chilled and cubed
salt and white pepper
squeeze of lemon juice

TO ASSEMBLE

225 g (8 oz) smoked salmon
40 g (1½ oz) butter, melted
dill sprigs and lemon
  wedges, to garnish

PREPARATION TIME
20-25 minutes, plus resting
COOKING TIME
10 minutes for sauce; 2 minutes
for pasta
FREEZING
Suitable: Uncooked pasta only,
in small quantities

970 CALS PER SERVING

1. To make the pasta, sift the flour and salt into a mound on a clean work surface and make a well in the centre.

2. Place the eggs, oil and dill in a blender or food processor and blend until smooth. Pour into the well.

3. Gradually mix the liquid into the flour, using the fingers of one hand, then bring the dough together.

4. On a clean surface, with clean hands, knead the pasta for 5-10 minutes until smooth and elastic. Wrap in cling film and allow to rest at room temperature for at least 30 minutes before rolling out.

5. Meanwhile, cut the smoked salmon into strips; cover and set aside.

6. Using a pasta machine or rolling pin, roll out the pasta dough very thinly in batches. Lay on floured tea towels and leave for 10 minutes to dry slightly. Cut the pasta into ribbons, either by machine or hand. To cut by hand, flour the pasta lightly and roll up like a Swiss roll, quickly slice with a sharp knife and unravel the tagliatelle. Leave to dry for 15 minutes on floured tea towels before cooking.

7. To make the butter sauce, finely chop the shallot and place in a small pan with 45 ml (3 tbsp) water and the vinegar. Boil until reduced to 30 ml (2 tbsp). Over a low heat, whisk in the butter, a piece at a time, until creamy and amalgamated: this process shouldn't take too long; do not allow to boil or the sauce will split. Season with salt and pepper, add the lemon juice and stir in the smoked salmon. Keep warm.

8. Bring a large pan of salted water to the boil and add the tagliatelle. Boil rapidly for 2 minutes or until *al dente*, then drain thoroughly. Toss the tagliatelle with the melted butter and divide between 4 warmed serving plates. Top with the smoked salmon in butter sauce. Garnish with sprigs of dill and lemon wedges. Serve at once.

TECHNIQUE

If you have a pasta machine, feed the pasta sheets through the tagliatelle attachment to cut the ribbons.

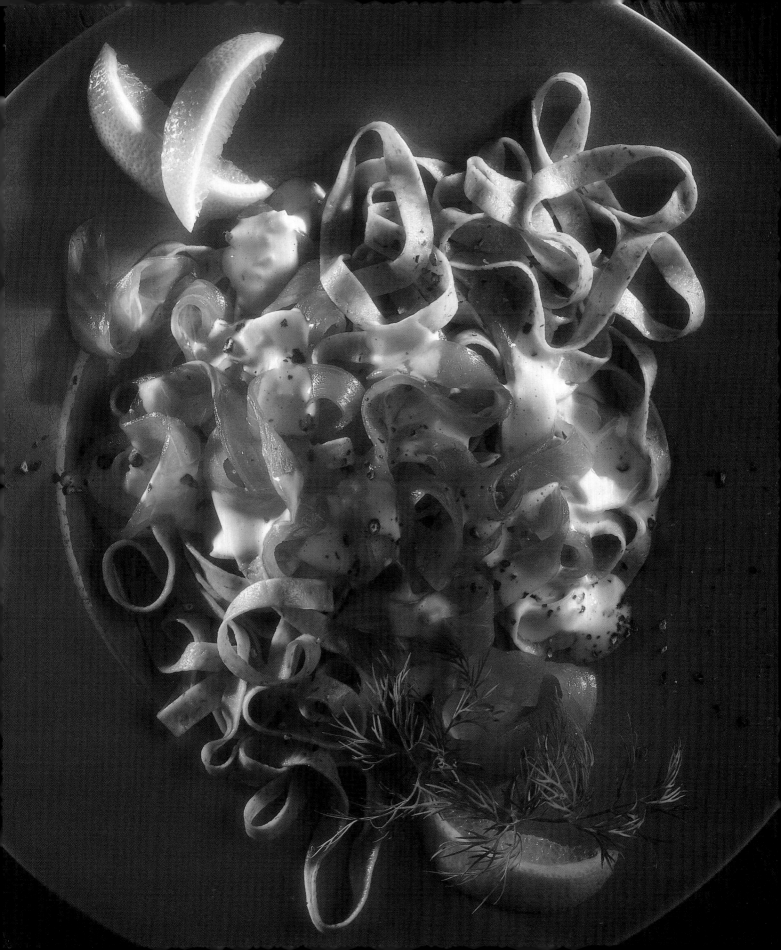

SALMON FILLET WITH A HERB CRUST

A crispy herb and breadcrumb crust flavoured with nuts and nutmeg coats tender salmon fillets. The salmon is cooked skin-side uppermost to prevent it drying out in the heat of the oven and the butter in the crust bastes the salmon as it cooks. Serve with a moist accompaniment, such as roasted tomatoes (see page 24).

SERVES 4

15 ml (1 tbsp) mixed
   peppercorns
4 salmon fillets with skin,
   each about 175 g (6 oz)
225 g (8 oz) fresh white
   breadcrumbs
90 ml (6 tbsp) mixed
   chopped fresh herbs, such
   as parsley, tarragon and
   chervil
finely grated rind of 1
   orange
1.25 ml (¼ tsp) freshly
   grated nutmeg
75 g (3 oz) shelled walnuts
125 g (4 oz) butter
salt and pepper
beaten egg yolk, for
   brushing
TO GARNISH
herb sprigs

PREPARATION TIME
15 minutes
COOKING TIME
15-20 minutes
FREEZING
Not suitable

875 CALS PER SERVING

1. Preheat the oven to 200°C (400°F) Mark 6. Crush the peppercorns finely, using a pestle and mortar. Rub the pepper evenly over the skinned side of the fish. Place the fish skin-side uppermost in a shallow baking dish.

2. Mix the breadcrumbs, herbs, orange rind and nutmeg together. Chop the nuts and add them to the breadcrumb mixture.

3. Melt the butter in a frying pan and stir in the breadcrumb mixture. Cook over a medium heat until the butter is absorbed and the crumbs are just beginning to brown. Season with salt and pepper.

4. Brush the salmon skin with beaten egg yolk and coat with the crumb mixture. Bake in the preheated oven for 15-20 minutes until the salmon is opaque and the crust is golden and crisp.

5. Transfer the salmon fillets to warmed serving plates. Serve immediately, together with any juices and extra crumbs, garnished with herb sprigs.

NOTE: Do not be alarmed by the quantity of butter in the herb crust. It will baste the fish during baking and form a sauce with the cooking juices.

VARIATION

Use a flavoured bread, like corn bread or walnut bread, to make the crumbs. Vary the nuts, or add a little grated fresh root ginger to the crumbs.

TECHNIQUE

Spoon the herb crumb mixture over the salmon fillets to coat evenly.

SALMON STEAKS WITH BASIL AND BALSAMIC VINEGAR

This pretty dish is very quick and easy to prepare. The salmon is grilled with balsamic vinegar which gives it a sweet-sour 'glaze'. The contrast of the hot salmon with the cool, firm tomatoes is sublime, especially when mingled with the basil oil. Crunchy-topped asparagus and courgettes (page 54) is an excellent accompaniment.

SERVES 4

4 salmon steaks, each about
  175 g (6 oz)
30 ml (2 tbsp) balsamic
  vinegar
10 ml (2 tsp) soy sauce
90 ml (6 tbsp) extra-virgin
  olive oil
40 g (1½ oz) fresh basil,
  stalks removed
8 ripe plum tomatoes (or
  other flavourful
  tomatoes)
30 ml (2 tbsp) chopped fresh
  chives
salt and pepper

PREPARATION TIME
30 minutes, plus marinating
COOKING TIME
8 minutes
FREEZING
Not suitable

540 CALS PER SERVING

1. Place the salmon steaks in a shallow non-metallic dish. Mix the balsamic vinegar and soy sauce together and pour over the salmon, turning to coat. Cover and leave to marinate in the refrigerator for 30 minutes.

2. Meanwhile, place the olive oil and basil in a food processor or blender and work until smooth. Pour into a bowl, cover and leave to infuse. (Do not make this too far in advance.)

3. Immerse the tomatoes in a bowl of boiling water for 10 seconds. Remove with a slotted spoon and plunge into cold water to stop the tomato flesh cooking. Slip off the skins, then halve the tomatoes and remove the seeds. Cut the flesh into fine dice and place in a bowl. Stir in the chives and season well with salt and pepper. Cover and set aside.

4. Preheat the grill. Lift the salmon out of the marinade and place on a foil-lined grill pan. Grill the salmon steaks for 4 minutes on each side, brushing liberally with the marinade once on each side. If necessary, whisk the basil oil briefly at this stage to re-combine.

5. Spoon a quarter of the tomato mixture onto each of four warmed serving plates and place a salmon steak on top.

Drizzle basil oil over each steak and spoon on any cooking juices. Serve immediately.

NOTE: Balsamic vinegar is widely available in delicatessens and large supermarkets. It is a dark brown, almost sweet-flavoured, vinegar which has been aged in casks to acquire its unique flavour. If unobtainable, sherry vinegar could be used instead.

TECHNIQUE

To make the basil oil, process the olive oil and basil together until smooth, then pour into a bowl and leave to infuse.

PINK TROUT WITH ALMOND AND HERB PURÉE

A sophisticated version of trout with almonds! Fresh pink trout is basted with paprika butter and grilled until crisp and russet-coloured. The accompanying purée of toasted almonds, parsley, garlic, Parmesan and olive oil has a superb earthy flavour. Potato and parsnip galette (page 62) goes well with this dish.

SERVES 4

4 pink-fleshed trout, each
  about 300 g (10 oz),
  cleaned
50 g (2 oz) butter
15 ml (1 tbsp) lemon juice
10 ml (2 tsp) paprika
75 g (3 oz) blanched whole
  almonds
1 garlic clove, peeled
30 ml (2 tbsp) freshly grated
  Parmesan cheese
50 g (2 oz) fresh parsley
  sprigs
150 ml (¼ pint) light olive
  oil
30 ml (2 tbsp) fromage frais
salt and pepper
TO GARNISH
parsley sprigs

PREPARATION TIME
20 minutes
COOKING TIME
10-14 minutes
FREEZING
Not suitable

745 CALS PER SERVING

1. Preheat the grill. Rinse the trout and pat dry.

2. Place the butter, lemon juice and paprika in a saucepan over a low heat until the butter is melted. With a sharp knife, make diagonal slashes on both sides of each trout. Lay the trout in a foil-lined grill pan and brush with the paprika butter.

3. Spread the almonds on a baking sheet and place under the grill for 2-3 minutes, turning frequently until toasted and golden. Place 50 g (2 oz) of the toasted almonds in a blender or food processor with the garlic, Parmesan, parsley, olive oil, fromage frais, salt and pepper. Blend until smooth. Roughly chop the remaining almonds and set aside.

4. Grill the trout for 5-7 minutes on each side or until opaque and cooked through, basting from time to time with the paprika butter.

5. Transfer the trout to warmed serving plates. Spoon a good dollop of toasted almond and herb purée onto each plate and scatter over the remaining toasted almonds. Garnish with sprigs of parsley and serve immediately.

NOTE: Pink-fleshed trout has the colour of salmon, but a much more delicate taste.

VARIATION

Replace the almonds with hazelnuts. Add 15 ml (1 tbsp) hazelnut oil to the olive oil.

TECHNIQUE

Using a sharp knife, score the trout diagonally on each side. Make the cuts about 1 cm (½ inch) deep to enable the heat to penetrate through, so the fish will cook more evenly.

ROASTED MONKFISH WITH MEDITERRANEAN VEGETABLES

This colourful, strongly-flavoured dish evokes all the savour of the Mediterranean. Monkfish is a closely textured fish that is perfect for roasting in this manner. Either buy ready-prepared monkfish or follow the step-by-step instructions for filleting on page 7.

SERVES 4

1 kg (2.2 lb) monkfish tail
   (on the bone), or two
   350 g (12 oz) monkfish
   fillets
3 fresh bay leaves
5 ml (1 tsp) fennel seeds
60 ml (4 tbsp) olive oil
few fresh thyme sprigs
salt and pepper
2 medium red peppers
3 ripe plum tomatoes (or
   other flavourful
   tomatoes)
1 medium aubergine
2 medium courgettes
30 ml (2 tbsp) capers,
   drained
45 ml (3 tbsp) chopped fresh
   parsley
4 garlic cloves (unpeeled)
45 ml (3 tbsp) lemon juice

PREPARATION TIME
30 minutes, plus marinating
COOKING TIME
25 minutes
FREEZING
Not suitable

375 CALS PER SERVING

1. Fillet the monkfish if necessary, then sandwich the two fillets together with the bay leaves and fennel seeds. Tie at 5 cm (2 inch) intervals with string.

2. Put the olive oil, thyme and a little pepper in a shallow non-metallic dish and add the monkfish, turning well to coat. Cover and leave to marinate in the refrigerator for at least 1 hour.

3. Preheat the oven to 220°C (425°F) Mark 7. Halve the red peppers and remove the core and seeds; cut each half into eight pieces. Halve the tomatoes lengthways, discard the seeds and cut the flesh into large dice. Trim the aubergine and cut into 2 cm (¾ inch) cubes. Cut the courgettes into similar-sized cubes. Chop the capers and mix with the parsley; cover and set aside.

4. Remove the fish from the marinade and pat dry. Pour 30 ml (2 tbsp) of the marinade into a heavy-based frying pan and heat until almost smoking. Add the monkfish and brown over a brisk heat for 2-3 minutes to seal. Transfer to a roasting rack.

5. In the same pan, quickly brown the unpeeled garlic and all of the vegetables except the tomatoes, using the remaining marinade. Transfer to a heavy-based

shallow baking dish and set the monkfish on top. Pour in the lemon juice. Bake in the oven for about 20 minutes, basting occasionally and turning the vegetables from time to time; add the tomatoes after 10 minutes.

6. Remove the string from the monkfish and slice thickly, discarding the bay leaves. Season the vegetables with salt and pepper to taste. Serve the monkfish on a bed of the roasted vegetables, garnished with the capers and parsley. Accompany with rice or new potatoes.

NOTE: Roasted garlic is soft and tastes sweetly nutty. Allow guests to squeeze it out of the skin and spread it on the fish.

TECHNIQUE

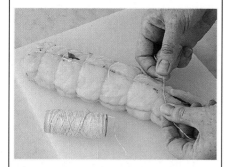

Place the bay leaves and fennel seeds between the two monkfish fillets and tie at 5 cm (2 inch) intervals with cotton string to secure.

FILO TURRETS OF SOLE

These 'leafy' parcels are a little tricky to make, but well worth the effort. The sole fillets are wrapped around a purée of prawns, ginger and dill, then enclosed in delicate leaves of filo pastry. To make the dish extra special, the turrets are served on a pool of ginger butter sauce – dotted with red jewels of salmon caviar.

SERVES 4

2 spring onions

1.25 cm (½ inch) piece fresh
   root ginger

225 g (8 oz) raw prawns
   (thawed if frozen), chilled

30 ml (2 tbsp) chopped fresh
   dill

1 egg white, lightly beaten

45 ml (3 tbsp) whipping
   cream

salt and pepper

4 double sole fillets

5 sheets filo pastry

75 g (3 oz) butter, melted

15 ml (1 tbsp) polenta or
   semolina flour

GINGER SAUCE

1 shallot

4 thin slices fresh root ginger

45 ml (3 tbsp) white wine
   vinegar

225 g (8 oz) unsalted butter,
   chilled and cubed

squeeze of lemon juice

TO GARNISH

salmon caviar

shredded spring onion

PREPARATION TIME
40 minutes
COOKING TIME
10-15 minutes
FREEZING
Not suitable

855 CALS PER SERVING

1. For the filling, chop the spring onions. Peel and grate the ginger. Place the prawns, onions, ginger and dill in a food processor and work to a paste.

2. With the machine running, pour in the egg white through the feeder tube and blend for 30 seconds. Add the cream in the same way and blend briefly until combined. Season.

3. Spread this paste evenly over each sole fillet and roll up from the thick end. Secure with a cocktail stick. Place in a shallow pan and pour in 150 ml (¼ pint) water. Slowly bring to a bare simmer, cover tightly and turn off the heat. Leave to partially cook in the residual heat for 10 minutes, then remove and drain on kitchen paper. Cool.

4. Cut the filo pastry into ten 20 cm (8 inch) squares and cover with a damp tea towel to prevent them drying out. Take two squares, brush with melted butter and place one on top of the other. Cut in half and place on top of each other, to form a rectangle of four layers. Cut out eight 2.5 cm (1 inch) squares – these will be the bases on which to sit the fish.

5. Preheat the oven to 200°C (400°F) Mark 6. Take the fish rolls and trim one edge of each flat, so they will stand up.

6. Butter one large square of filo. Place a small filo square in the middle and sprinkle it with polenta. Place a fish roll on top, then bring the filo up and around it, twisting to secure. Frill out the filo tops and place on a baking sheet. Repeat with the remaining fish and filo. Drizzle the parcels with butter and bake in the oven for 10-15 minutes until crisp and golden.

7. Meanwhile, make the sauce. Finely chop the shallot and place in a small pan with the ginger, 45 ml (3 tbsp) water and the vinegar. Boil until reduced to 30 ml (2 tbsp). Discard the ginger. Over a low heat, whisk in the butter, a piece at a time, until creamy and amalgamated. Do not allow to boil. Add the lemon juice and seasoning to taste.

8. Serve two 'turrets' on each warmed plate on a pool of ginger butter sauce. Garnish with the salmon caviar and spring onion shreds.

TECHNIQUE

Twist the tops of the filo bundles to secure, then frill out the edges attractively.

BEEF FILLET WITH A WALNUT CRUST

Fillet of beef may seem a bit extravagant, but it is so deliciously rich, you don't need much – especially if you serve it with a potato and parsnip galette (page 62) or sweet potato and chestnut cakes (page 58). The piece of fillet is cut into thick steaks which are topped with a savoury mixture of walnuts and anchovies, and popped into the oven at the last moment. A very easy dish – all prepared in advance!

SERVES 6

350 g (12 oz) walnut pieces

125 g (4 oz) pickled walnuts, drained (see note)

50 g (2 oz) can anchovies, drained

2 garlic cloves, peeled

15 ml (1 tbsp) thick soy sauce

about 45 ml (3 tbsp) olive oil

salt and pepper

1-1.1 kg (2¼-2½ lb) piece fillet of beef, trimmed

30 ml (2 tbsp) sunflower or corn oil

60 ml (4 tbsp) white wine

300 ml (½ pint) well-flavoured beef stock

TO SERVE

4 large radicchio leaves (optional)

60 ml (4 tbsp) chopped fresh parsley

parsley sprigs, to garnish

PREPARATION TIME
30 minutes
COOKING TIME
15-20 minutes
FREEZING
Not suitable

750 CALS PER SERVING

1. Roughly chop both types of walnut together; set aside one half. Place the other half of the chopped nuts in a blender or food processor with the anchovies, garlic, soy sauce and olive oil. Blend until smooth. Stir in the reserved walnuts and season with salt and pepper; the paste should be quite thick and lumpy.

2. With a sharp knife, slice the fillet into six thick steaks. Heat the oil in a heavy-based frying pan until almost smoking. Fry the steaks, one at a time, very quickly on all sides to brown and seal. Allow to cool. Top each steak thickly with the anchovy and walnut paste. Cover and refrigerate until ready to cook.

3. To make the gravy, deglaze the frying pan with the wine, stirring to scrape up the sediment. Add the beef stock, bring to the boil and boil steadily for 2-3 minutes until reduced slightly. Check the seasoning. Pour into a bowl and cool. Cover and refrigerate until needed.

4. Remove the steaks from the refrigerator 15-20 minutes before cooking to allow them to come to room temperature. Preheat the oven to 200°C (400°F) Mark 6.

5. Place the steaks on a baking sheet. Bake in the oven for 10-15 minutes, depending on thickness and preference for rare or medium cooked steaks. Meanwhile reheat the gravy in a small pan.

6. Serve the steaks on warmed plates as soon as they are cooked. If desired, place each one on a radicchio leaf. Sprinkle with plenty of chopped parsley and garnish with extra parsley sprigs. Serve with the gravy.

NOTE: Pickled walnuts are available in jars from larger supermarkets and delicatessens. If unobtainable, simply increase the quantity of walnut pieces by 125 g (4 oz) and add 15 ml (1 tbsp) wine vinegar to the blender.

TECHNIQUE

Top each steak thickly with the anchovy and walnut paste.

LAMB CUTLETS WITH MINTED CUCUMBER SALSA

Juicy and tender spring lamb is roasted to golden crispness on the outside while rosy pink on the inside. The sauce is made from the pan juices, flavoured with orange and a hint of mint jelly. Serve with dreamy smooth buttery mashed potatoes mixed with spring onions and black pepper, plus seasonal vegetables. Have the lamb sealed and ready to pop in the oven just before you start the meal.

SERVES 6

three 7-bone racks of spring
   lamb
30 ml (2 tbsp) brandy
salt and pepper
a little sunflower oil, for
   brushing
SALSA
1 medium cucumber
2 pickled dill cucumbers
1 small sweet red onion
45 ml (3 tbsp) chopped fresh
   mint
SAUCE
150 ml (¼ pint) medium dry
   white wine
10 ml (2 tsp) flour
finely grated rind and juice
   of 2 oranges
45 ml (3 tbsp) mint jelly
TO GARNISH
mint sprigs

PREPARATION TIME
35 minutes
COOKING TIME
20-30 minutes
FREEZING
Not suitable

400 CALS PER SERVING

1. Trim the racks of fat if not already done (see page 8), leaving a very fine layer on the outside to baste the meat during cooking. Rub with the brandy and seasoning. Cover and leave in a cool place for 30 minutes.

2. To make the salsa, peel the cucumber, if preferred. Halve the cucumber lengthways and scoop out the seeds. Cut the flesh into fine dice. Finely dice the dill pickles. Peel and finely dice the onion. Mix all these ingredients together and stir in the mint. Season with salt and pepper to taste. Cover and chill.

3. Preheat the oven to 200°C (400°F) Mark 6. Stand the rack of lamb in a roasting tin. Brush with a little oil and roast in the preheated oven for 20-30 minutes, depending on how pink you like your lamb. Remove from the oven and transfer to a warm dish. Cover with foil and leave to rest in a warm place for 10 minutes before carving – this makes the lamb more juicy and easier to carve.

4. Meanwhile make the sauce. Set the roasting pan over a medium heat and pour in the wine. Bring to the boil, scraping up the sediment off the bottom of the pan. Boil until well reduced, then whisk in the flour. Cook, stirring, for 1

minute then add the orange rind, juice and mint jelly. Bring to the boil, then simmer for 2-3 minutes until syrupy. If too thick add a little more wine or water. Season with salt and pepper to taste. Strain if you like, but the bits add character! Pour into a warmed jug.

5. Cut the lamb into cutlets, allowing 3 per person. Arrange on warmed dinner plates. Spoon a little salsa on top of each cutlet and pour a little sauce around them. Garnish with mint sprigs and serve the remaining sauce separately.

NOTE: It is essential to use well-trimmed lamb for this recipe. If you don't remove the outer layer of fat the meat will take longer to cook.

TECHNIQUE

If the rack of lamb is not ready-trimmed, pull off the thick outer layer of fat.

LAMB MEATBALLS WITH DILL SAUCE

Cinnamon adds a hint of spice to these delicate fine-textured meatballs, which are served with a creamy wine and dill-flavoured sauce. If fresh dill is unobtainable you will find that dried dill weed – with its concentrated flavour – is an excellent substitute.

SERVES 6

6 spring onions

175 g (6 oz) unsmoked
    rindless streaky bacon

1 garlic clove

pinch of ground cinnamon

700 g (1½ lb) lean minced
    lamb

salt and pepper

45 ml (3 tbsp) olive oil

450 ml (¾ pint) dry white
    wine

60 ml (4 tbsp) chopped fresh
    dill or 20 ml (2 tsp) dried
    dill weed

300 ml (½ pint) double
    cream

2 egg yolks

TO GARNISH

dill sprigs and lemon wedges

PREPARATION TIME
30 minutes
COOKING TIME
1 hour 10 minutes
FREEZING
Suitable, without cream. Stir in
cream just before serving

650 CALS PER SERVING

1. Trim the spring onions; roughly chop the bacon; peel the garlic. Place the spring onions, bacon, garlic and cinnamon in a food processor and blend until almost smooth. Add the minced lamb and plenty of salt and pepper. Process until well mixed and smooth.

2. With wet hands, shape the mixture into 30-36 even-sized balls. Keep wetting your hands to prevent sticking.

3. Preheat the oven to 180°C (350°F) Mark 4. Heat the oil in a large frying pan and brown the meatballs in batches, then transfer to a shallow ovenproof dish. Pour the wine into the frying pan and bring to the boil, scraping up any sediment from the bottom of the pan. Pour over the meatballs, cover and bake in the preheated oven for 1 hour.

4. Pour the cooking liquid into a saucepan; cover the meatballs and keep warm. Bring the liquid to the boil and boil rapidly until reduced to 300 ml (½ pint). Lower the heat and stir in the dill, cream and egg yolks. Stir over a gentle heat for about 10 minutes or until slightly thickened; do not allow to boil. Taste and adjust the seasoning.

5. Transfer the meatballs to warmed serving plates and spoon the sauce over them. Garnish with dill sprigs and lemon wedges. Serve with boiled new potatoes or buttered noodles.

VARIATION

Use lean minced pork instead of lamb and tarragon in place of the dill.

TECHNIQUE

With dampened hands, roll each piece of mixture in the palm of your hand to form an even-shaped ball.

PORK FILLET WITH GARLIC AND PEPPER STUFFING

Pork is delicious cooked with sweet peppers and garlic. Ring the changes by using yellow or orange peppers, but avoid green ones, as they can be a little bitter. Pork fillet is beautifully tender and needs very little cooking – so don't be tempted to overcook it. I like to serve this dish with sweet potato and chestnut cakes (page 58), and a green vegetable. As it is quite rich and filling, choose a light starter and pudding to balance the meal.

SERVES 6

2 large red peppers

6 large garlic cloves

1 medium onion

60-90 ml (4-6 tbsp)
    sunflower oil

50 g (2 oz) pine nuts

salt and pepper

3 pork fillets (tenderloins),
    each about 350 g (12 oz)

300 ml (½ pint) medium dry
    white wine

300 ml (½ pint) cider

large pinch of saffron
    threads

2.5 ml (½ tsp) mild chilli
    seasoning

PREPARATION TIME
35 minutes
COOKING TIME
40-45 minutes
FREEZING
Not suitable

440 CALS PER SERVING

1. Halve, core and seed the peppers, then dice. Peel and chop the garlic roughly. Peel and finely chop the onion. Heat 30-45 ml (2-3 tbsp) of oil in a saucepan and add the garlic and onion. Cook gently for 5 minutes or until softened and turning golden. Stir in the peppers and pine nuts and cook for a further 5 minutes. Season with salt and pepper.

2. Slice each pork fillet along its length without cutting all the way through, then open out like a book. Place the pork fillets between sheets of greaseproof paper and lightly flatten with a rolling pin; don't overdo this, otherwise the meat will be too thin.

3. Spoon the pepper and garlic mixture down the middle of each fillet. Bring the sides of the meat over the filling to enclose it and carefully tie the stuffed pork fillet at 2.5 cm (1 inch) intervals with cotton string.

4. Preheat the oven to 190°C (375°F) Mark 5. Heat the remaining oil in a shallow flameproof baking dish and brown the pork fillets all over. Mix the wine and cider with the saffron and chilli and pour over the meat. Cover with foil and bake in the preheated oven for 25 minutes. Remove the foil and roast, uncovered,

for a further 10-15 minutes to brown the meat, and reduce the sauce slightly.

5. Transfer the meat to a warmed serving dish with a slotted spoon and keep warm. Place the baking dish over a medium heat and scrape up the sediment in the bottom to amalgamate with the juices. Season with salt and pepper. Bring to the boil to reduce the liquid a little, then pour into a warmed sauceboat. To serve, slice the meat thickly, arrange on warmed serving plates and pour over a little sauce. Serve the remaining sauce separately.

NOTE: Use a generous pinch of turmeric if you do not have any saffron.

TECHNIQUE

Split the pork fillets lengthwise without cutting right through, then open out like a book.

CHICKEN BREASTS WITH SPINACH AND RICOTTA

Tender chicken breasts are stuffed with a well-seasoned ricotta filling, then wrapped in fresh spinach leaves and poached in wine until tender. The cooking juices are reduced to form a delicate sauce which is 'mounted' with a little butter for gloss. A pale and pretty dish – full of fresh, clean flavours – which is ideal served with crunchy-topped asparagus and courgettes (page 54).

SERVES 4

4 boneless chicken breasts, skinned
50 g (2 oz) frozen chopped spinach, thawed
175 g (6 oz) ricotta cheese
60 ml (4 tbsp) freshly grated Parmesan cheese
freshly grated nutmeg
salt and pepper
8 large fresh spinach leaves
150 ml (¼ pint) dry white wine
300 ml (½ pint) chicken stock
50 g (2 oz) butter, chilled and diced

PREPARATION TIME
30 minutes
COOKING TIME
30-40 minutes
FREEZING
Not suitable

400 CALS PER SERVING

1. Using a sharp knife, make a deep horizontal slit in each chicken breast through the thicker side, to make a pocket.

2. Squeeze the moisture out of the thawed spinach, then place in a bowl. Add the ricotta, Parmesan and plenty of nutmeg, salt and pepper. Mix well, then spoon the filling evenly into the chicken pockets.

3. Trim the stems from the fresh spinach. Bring a pan of salted water to the boil and add the spinach leaves. Immediately remove with a slotted spoon and plunge into a bowl of cold water to set the colour and prevent further cooking. Wrap two spinach leaves around each chicken breast. Tie with thin cotton string to secure.

4. Lay the chicken breasts in a wide shallow pan or flameproof casserole and pour in the wine and stock. Bring to the boil, lower the heat, cover and simmer gently for 30-40 minutes until cooked. Remove the chicken breasts from the pan with a slotted spoon and keep warm.

5. Boil the cooking liquid rapidly until reduced by half. Take off the heat and whisk in the cubed butter, to enrich the sauce and give it a shine. Taste and adjust the seasoning.

6. To serve, slice the chicken breasts and arrange on warmed serving plates with a little sauce. Serve the remaining sauce separately.

NOTE: Another type of curd cheese or soft cream cheese can be used in place of the ricotta.

TECHNIQUE

Cut a deep pocket in each chicken breast, then spoon in the spinach and ricotta filling, dividing it equally between them.

DUCK BREASTS WITH RÖSTI AND APPLE

Rosy pink, tender slices of 'roasted' duck breast are served on golden apple and potato cakes and accompanied by sautéed caramelised apple slices. The method used to cook the duck breasts encourages most of the fat to run out and the skin becomes deliciously crisp and brown. If possible buy the large French *magrets* – one of these easily serves two. Otherwise you will need four standard sized duck breasts.

SERVES 4

2 large duck breast fillets,
  each about 350 g (12 oz),
  or 4 medium duck breast
  fillets (at room
  temperature)
salt and pepper
15 ml (1 tbsp) red wine
  vinegar
60 ml (4 tbsp) apple juice
RÖSTI
2 large old potatoes, about
  450 g (1 lb) total weight
1 dessert apple
2 fresh sage leaves
oil, for frying
TO GARNISH
sautéed apple slices
sage sprigs

PREPARATION TIME
30 minutes
COOKING TIME
20-25 minutes
FREEZING
Not suitable

430 CALS PER SERVING

1. Use a sharp knife to score through the skin side of the duck. Rub with salt and pepper. Leave at room temperature for 15 minutes.

2. To make the rösti, peel and finely grate the potatoes and apple. Squeeze out as much moisture as possible and place in a bowl. Chop the sage and mix with the potato and apple. Season well with salt and pepper.

3. Preheat the oven to 150°C (300°F) Mark 2. Heat 15 ml (1 tbsp) oil in a small heavy-based frying pan. Place 2 large tablespoonfuls of the potato mixture in the pan, pressing down hard with a fish slice. Cook for 2 minutes or until golden brown on the underside; turn over and cook until crisp and golden. Remove and drain on kitchen paper. Repeat with the remaining mixture until you have at least 8 rösti. Keep warm in the oven while cooking the duck.

4. Preheat a heavy flameproof casserole. Add the duck breasts skin-side down and cook over a medium heat for 7-10 minutes depending on size, without moving them; the fat that runs out will prevent them sticking. Turn the breasts over and cook for 3-4 minutes, depending on size.

5. Using a slotted spoon, transfer the duck breasts to a warmed serving dish. Cover and leave in the warm oven for 10 minutes to relax and become evenly 'rosy' inside. Meanwhile pour of all the fat from the pan. Add the wine vinegar and apple juice. Bring to the boil and reduce slightly.

6. To serve, place two rösti on each warmed serving plate. Slice the duck thickly and arrange evenly on top of the rösti. Spoon on the sauce and serve immediately, garnished with sautéed apple slices and sage.

TECHNIQUE

Score through the skin of each duck breast on the diagonal, using a sharp knife. This encourages the fat to run out and the skin to crisp on cooking.

CHAR-GRILLED SPATCHCOCK POUSSINS

Spatchcocked poussins make an unusual change from roast chicken. The poussin or baby chicken is split and flattened enabling it to be grilled evenly. Ready-prepared spatchcocked poussins are widely available in supermarkets, but you can always prepare them yourself if preferred (see step-by-step instructions on page 9). Brushed with a honey and lemon glaze, the skin becomes shiny, partly charred and crisp – with a lemony tang. Stir-fried summer vegetables (page 60) are an excellent accompaniment.

SERVES 4

2 or 4 ready-prepared
  spatchcock poussins (see
  note)
finely grated rind and juice
  of 1 lemon
60 ml (4 tbsp) thin honey
30 ml (2 tbsp) Dijon
  mustard
30 ml (2 tbsp) dark soy
  sauce
5 ml (1 tsp) mild paprika
salt and pepper

PREPARATION TIME
15 minutes
COOKING TIME
20-30 minutes
FREEZING
Not suitable

330 CALS PER SERVING

1. Preheat the grill to medium. Place the poussins skin-side down on a grill rack.

2. In a bowl, mix the lemon juice with the honey, mustard, soy sauce, paprika and seasoning to make the glaze.

3. Brush the poussins all over with the glaze and grill for 10 minutes, brushing with more glaze as necessary. Turn over carefully and brush with glaze. Grill for 10-20 minutes until the poussins are cooked through and the juices from the thigh run clear, not pink (see note). The skin will be well-charred while the meat underneath should be perfectly tender.

4. Remove any skewers from the poussins. If using larger poussins, split in two along the length of the breast bone. Serve the poussins with any pan juices poured over, accompanied by stir-fried summer vegetables.

NOTE: If you buy small poussins, you will need to allow one per person. Larger poussins will serve two, but may take longer to cook through. If necessary lower the grill pan to prevent the skin from over-blackening.

VARIATION

In place of poussins, use chicken joints or even chicken breasts – corn-fed ones have a particularly good flavour.

TECHNIQUE

Brush the poussins all over with the lemon and honey glaze before – and during – grilling.

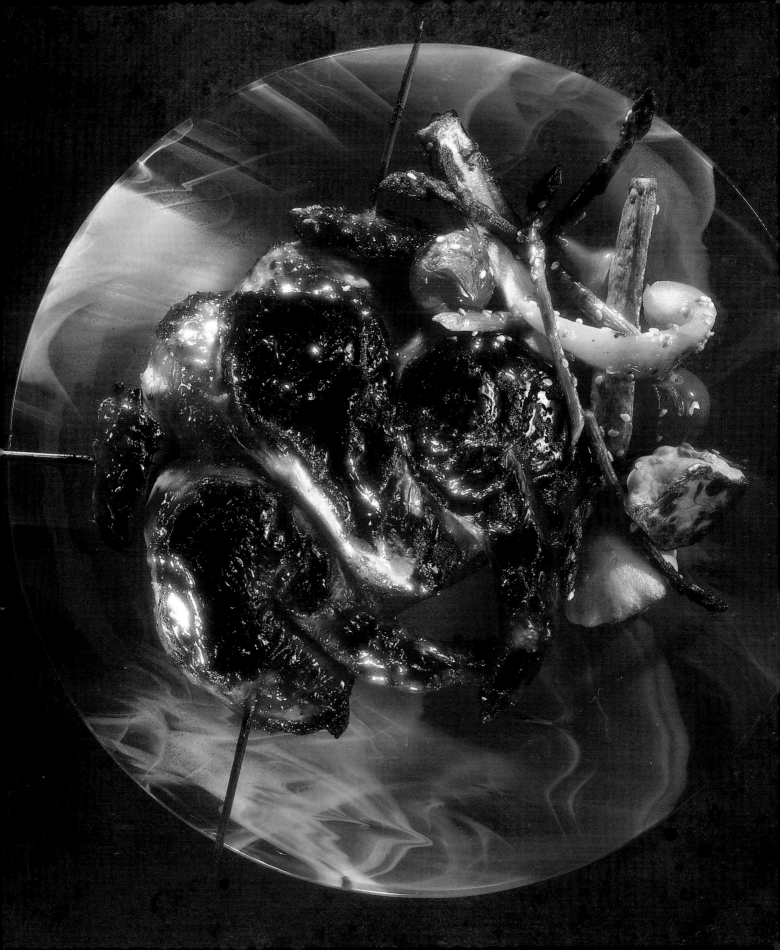

BITTER GREEN SALAD WITH CITRUS DRESSING

A delicious crunchy, slightly peppery salad to accompany rich meats, or to serve as a separate salad course. The piquant dressing adds a mellow sweetness to the sharp leaves – but remember to apply it just before serving otherwise the salad will become limp. Bitter leaves are becoming more readily available in supermarkets today – look out for new varieties and experiment!

SERVES 4

**225 g (8 oz) mixed bitter
salad leaves, such as
rocket, watercress,
batavia, sorrel, young
spinach**
CITRUS DRESSING
1 orange
1 lime
30 ml (2 tbsp) sunflower oil
15 ml (1 tbsp) walnut oil
**15 ml (1 tbsp) dark soy
sauce**
15 ml (1 tbsp) thin honey
salt and pepper

PREPARATION TIME
15 minutes
COOKING TIME
Nil
FREEZING
Not suitable

125 CALS PER SERVING

1. Wash all the salad leaves and tear into smaller pieces if necessary. Spin dry in a salad spinner, then transfer to a plastic bag with any water still clinging to the leaves. Store in the refrigerator for about 30 minutes to crisp up the salad.

2. To make the dressing, finely grate the rind from the orange and lime. Squeeze the juice from both fruit. Place 15 ml (1 tbsp) each grated rind in a small bowl with 30 ml (2 tbsp) orange juice and 15 ml (1 tbsp) lime juice. Add the oils, soy sauce and honey, and whisk well. Taste and check the seasoning. Just before serving the salad, strain the dressing through a fine sieve.

3. To serve, place the salad leaves in a bowl and pour over the dressing. Toss well and serve immediately.

NOTE: Rocket is expensive to buy, but grows like a weed in the garden. Try planting some – it will even grow in a window box!

TECHNIQUE

Wash the salad leaves under cold running water and tear any larger ones into smaller pieces.

VARIATION

Make the salad with chicory leaves and radicchio for a more colourful version. Add sprigs of herbs, such as basil, chervil, dill and tarragon.

CRUNCHY-TOPPED ASPARAGUS AND COURGETTES

This is a really quick and simple way of serving seasonal vegetables. The crunchy breadcrumb and Parmesan topping provides an excellent contrast to the melting texture of the asparagus and courgettes. Try it with other vegetables too, such as broccoli or cauliflower.

SERVES 4-6

225 g (8 oz) thin asparagus
225 g (8 oz) baby courgettes
salt and pepper
125 g (4 oz) butter
175 g (6 oz) fresh white
    breadcrumbs
50 g (2 oz) freshly grated
    Parmesan cheese

PREPARATION TIME
15 minutes
COOKING TIME
5-6 minutes
FREEZING
Not suitable

445-300 CALS PER SERVING

1. Trim the asparagus and cut into 5 cm (2 inch) lengths. Cut the courgettes into quarters lengthways. Bring a pan of salted water to the boil. Drop in the asparagus and courgettes, return to the boil and cook for 3 minutes. Drain and refresh immediately in cold water to stop the cooking. Remove and drain on kitchen paper.

2. Heat the butter in a frying pan and fry the breadcrumbs until lightly golden and crisp. Stir in the Parmesan cheese.

3. Preheat the grill. Place the asparagus and courgettes in a warmed shallow flameproof dish. Cover thickly with the crumbs and place under the grill for 2-3 minutes or until the topping is golden and the vegetables are heated through. Serve immediately.

VARIATION

Replace the asparagus and/or courgettes with any other green vegetable – try broccoli florets, cauliflower, French beans, or even carrots, but be sure to half-cook them before adding the topping.

TECHNIQUE

To quickly stop the vegetables cooking, remove from the boiling water and briefly immerse in a bowl of cold water. The easiest way to do this is to contain the vegetables in a blanching basket during cooking.

GRILLED CHICORY AND RADICCHIO WITH ORANGE

Grilling the chicory and radicchio transforms them by caramelising the juices — and the addition of creamy, fresh British goat's cheese gives this recipe true dinner-party status! Any other cheese will do, but the goat's cheese seems to have a special affinity with bitter leaves like chicory and radicchio. Serve this accompaniment with roast or grilled meats or poultry.

SERVES 4

2 plump heads of chicory
1 large firm head of
  radicchio
1 orange
olive oil, for basting
125 g (4 oz) fresh goat's
  cheese
a little chopped fresh or
  dried thyme
pepper
30 ml (2 tbsp) pine nuts

PREPARATION TIME
15 minutes
COOKING TIME
About 10 minutes
FREEZING
Not suitable

230 CALS PER SERVING

1. Cut the chicory in half lengthways. Cut the radicchio into quarters. Over a bowl to catch the juice, peel the orange of all pith and cut into segments, discarding the membrane.

2. Preheat the grill to high. Place the chicory and radicchio in a grill pan, cut side up, and brush liberally with olive oil. Cook under the grill, as near to the heat as possible, for about 3-4 minutes until just beginning to char and soften. Turn, baste with more olive oil and cook for a further 2-3 minutes.

3. Carefully turn the chicory and radicchio again. Arrange the orange segments on top and sprinkle with the reserved orange juice. Crumble the goat's cheese on top. Brush with oil, sprinkle with thyme and season with pepper. Grill until the cheese bubbles and begins to brown. The chicory will be very soft, so carefully transfer it to warmed plates. Alternatively, transfer to a flameproof serving dish before adding the cheese, then grill in the dish.

4. Meanwhile toast the pine nuts in a dry pan over moderate heat, shaking the pan constantly, until evenly golden. Sprinkle the toasted nuts over the grilled chicory and radicchio, to serve.

NOTE: The chicory and radicchio will change colour, but don't worry — they will taste delicious — as long as you use olive oil for basting.

VARIATION

Omit the goat's cheese and top with orange slices instead of segments.

TECHNIQUE

Peel the orange (as you would an apple) over a bowl to catch the juice, making sure you remove all of the white pith.

SWEET POTATO AND CHESTNUT CAKES WITH SPRING ONIONS

Chestnuts and sweet potatoes have a natural affinity as you will discover on tasting these unusual patties. Avoid using canned chestnuts in brine – they will be too watery. The crisp-fried cakes are best served with game and rich dark meat dishes. Alternatively try serving them on their own with a tomato sauce.

SERVES 4-6

450 g (1 lb) sweet potatoes
(see note)
225 g (8 oz) vacuum-packed
chestnuts
6 spring onions
75 g (3 oz) butter
30 ml (2 tbsp) chopped fresh
parsley
2.5 ml (½ tsp) ground mace
salt and pepper
flour, for coating
1 (size 1) egg, beaten
125 g (4 oz) fresh white
breadcrumbs
sunflower oil, for shallow-
frying
TO GARNISH
parsley sprigs

PREPARATION TIME
30 minutes, plus chilling
COOKING TIME
30 minutes
FREEZING
Suitable: Stage 4

570-380 CALS PER SERVING

1. Peel the sweet potatoes and cut into large chunks. Place in a steamer and steam for 15-20 minutes until tender. Remove the basket from the steamer and allow the potatoes to rest for 2-3 minutes to allow excess moisture to evaporate.

2. Place the potatoes and chestnuts in a bowl and mash until smooth. Trim and slice the spring onions.

3. Heat the butter in a frying pan and add the spring onions. Fry for 1 minute until beginning to soften, then add to the potato with the parsley and mix well. Season with the mace, and salt and pepper to taste. Work the ingredients until the mixture comes together.

4. Divide the mixture into eight and roll each portion into a ball. Flatten each one to make a thick cake. Transfer to a baking sheet and chill in the refrigerator for at least 30 minutes.

5. Season a little flour and use to lightly coat the cakes. Dip each one into beaten egg and finally coat with the breadcrumbs. Chill in the refrigerator for 30 minutes to set.

6. Heat a 1 cm (½ inch) depth of oil in a frying pan until a breadcrumb dropped into the pan sizzles in 30 seconds. Fry the cakes in batches on both sides until golden. Drain on kitchen paper. Serve immediately, garnished with parsley.

NOTE: There are two kinds of sweet potato – one has a purply skin and orange flesh, the other has a brown skin and white flesh. Both taste good but the orange-fleshed variety has the edge.

VARIATION

For a less rich version, use plain mashed potato instead of the sweet potato.

TECHNIQUE

Roll each piece into a ball in the palm of your hand, then flatten to form a cake.

STIR-FRIED SUMMER VEGETABLES

This colourful stir-fry has the sweet-sour taste of balsamic vinegar which brings out the earthy sweetness of the vegetables. Those suggested here are just a selection of the vegetables available throughout the summer: try other combinations, but always blanch or par-cook harder ones first.

SERVES 4-6

1 large yellow pepper
125 g (4 oz) baby courgettes
125 g (4 oz) patty pan
    squashes (optional)
125 g (4 oz) baby carrots
125 g (4 oz) fine asparagus
2 garlic cloves
15 ml (1 tbsp) vegetable oil
15 ml (1 tbsp) olive oil
125 g (4 oz) cherry
    tomatoes
75 ml (3 fl oz) chicken or
    vegetable stock or canned
    consommé (see note)
salt and pepper
30 ml (2 tbsp) balsamic or
    sherry vinegar
5 ml (1 tbsp) sesame oil
TO GARNISH
15 ml (1 tbsp) toasted
    sesame seeds

PREPARATION TIME
15 minutes
COOKING TIME
7-8 minutes
FREEZING
Not suitable

160-110 CALS PER SERVING

1. Halve the pepper, remove the core and seeds, then cut into long triangular shapes. Halve the courgettes lengthways. If using patty pans, cut them in half. Trim the carrots and peel if necessary, leaving on a tuft of stalk. Trim the asparagus spears. Peel and roughly chop the garlic.

2. Bring a pan of salted water to the boil. Add the yellow pepper and carrots and blanch for 2 minutes, then remove with a slotted spoon and plunge into a bowl of cold water to stop the cooking and preserve the colour. Drain well on kitchen paper.

3. Heat a wok or deep frying pan until smoking, swirl in the vegetable and olive oils and add the garlic. Stir-fry for 20 seconds, then add all the vegetables and stir-fry for 1 minute. Pour in the stock and season with salt and pepper. Stir-fry for 3-4 minutes until the vegetables are just tender.

4. Sprinkle over the balsamic vinegar and sesame oil, stir and transfer to a warmed serving dish. Sprinkle with the sesame seeds and serve immediately.

NOTE: Canned consommé is a good substitute for small amounts of stock as it imparts plenty of flavour and 'body'.

VARIATION

For a winter vegetable stir-fry, use equal quantities of cauliflower florets, broccoli florets and carrot sticks, plus 2-3 spring onions, sliced, and a little chopped fresh root ginger.

TECHNIQUE

Toss the vegetables constantly over a high heat to ensure they cook quickly, retaining their colour and a crisp texture.

POTATO PARSNIP GALETTE

This golden cake of butter-basted potatoes and sweet parsnips with a hint of honey and lemon is a perfect partner to roasts and game dishes. It is really important to clarify the butter – as it lends a wonderful colour to the potatoes and intensifies the flavour.

SERVES 6

900 g (2 lb) firm potatoes,
    such as Desirée, Romano,
    Estima or Wilja
225 g (8 oz) young parsnips
175 g (6 oz) unsalted butter
60 ml (4 tbsp) thin honey
30 ml (2 tbsp) lemon juice
freshly grated nutmeg
salt and pepper

PREPARATION TIME
25 minutes
COOKING TIME
45 minutes
FREEZING
Not suitable

380 CALS PER SERVING

1. Preheat the oven to 200°C (400°F) Mark 6. Peel the potatoes and parsnips. Slice them very thinly either by hand, with a mandoline, or in a food processor. Do not rinse the potatoes to remove the starch as it is needed to help the potato slices stick together. Divide the potatoes into three equal portions. Don't worry if they discolour.

2. To clarify the butter, slowly melt it in a small pan, then skim off any white residue or foam; keep warm. Melt the honey and lemon juice together in a small pan; keep warm.

3. Pour 30 ml (2 tbsp) butter into a heavy 20 cm (8 inch) non-stick frying pan, suitable for oven use (see note). Layer one third of the potatoes over the bottom of the pan in neat overlapping circles, seasoning well.

4. Lay half the sliced parsnips over the potato layer. Brush with honey and lemon juice and season with nutmeg, salt and pepper.

5. Cover with another third of the potato slices, brushing with butter and seasoning well as you go. Layer the remaining parsnips on top. Brush with the remaining honey and lemon juice, and season with nutmeg, salt and pepper. Finish with the remaining potato slices, brushing with butter and seasoning. Pour over any remaining butter.

6. Place the pan over a medium heat and cook carefully for about 5 minutes or until the underside begins to turn golden brown. Test by carefully lifting up the edge with a palette knife.

7. Press the potatoes down firmly and cover with a lid or buttered kitchen foil. Bake for 40-45 minutes or until the potatoes and parsnips are tender when pierced with a sharp knife and the underside is a deep golden brown.

8. Loosen the galette with a palette knife. Place a warmed serving plate over the pan and quickly invert the galette onto the dish. Serve immediately.

NOTE: Ideally you need a non-stick frying pan with an integral metal handle which can therefore be placed in the oven. Alternatively, use a moule á manqué pan instead, buttering it well.

TECHNIQUE

Layer the potato slices over the parsnips in neat, overlapping circles.

STEAMED BASIL AND MUSTARD SEED RICE

Wonderfully fragrant, this rice is a little sticky, but great for mopping up juices. It goes equally well with fish, meat or game. Black mustard seeds impart a nutty flavour to the rice without being too hot. You can, however, use yellow mustard seeds as an alternative – for a hotter flavour.

SERVES 4

225 g (8 oz) basmati rice
12 large basil leaves
30 ml (2 tbsp) sunflower oil
30 ml (2 tbsp) black
   mustard seeds
5 ml (1 tsp) salt
TO GARNISH
basil leaves

PREPARATION TIME
10 minutes
COOKING TIME
25 minutes
FREEZING
Not suitable

270 CALS PER SERVING

1. Wash the rice in several changes of cold water or in a sieve under cold running water until the water runs clear. Drain well. Shred the basil leaves or tear into pieces.

2. Heat the oil in a medium non-stick saucepan and add the mustard seeds. Cook for a few minutes until the seeds start to pop.

3. Stir in the rice, salt and 300 ml (½ pint) water. Bring to the boil, stir, then boil rapidly until the water has evaporated and there are steam holes all over the surface.

4. Stir in all but 15 ml (1 tbsp) of the basil and cover very tightly, so no steam can escape. Set on a simmering mat (see note) over a very low heat for 15 minutes for the rice to swell. Fluff up with a fork, adding the reserved basil. Serve immediately, garnished with basil leaves.

NOTE: A simmering mat is used here to ensure the heat is *very* low and evenly distributed. You can obtain one of these mats from a cookshop or hardware store. If you do not have one make sure the heat is kept to a minimum and add a little more water if necessary to prevent the rice sticking.

VARIATION

Use multi-grain rice, but allow longer to cook: fast boil with 450 ml (¾ pint) water until evaporated, then continue as above.

TECHNIQUE

Wash the basmati rice thoroughly, running the grains through your fingers, to remove excess starch.

TIRAMISU TORTE

An outrageously rich cheesecake with an irresistible soft gooey texture, based on the delicious ingredients of Tiramisu – coffee, mascarpone, chocolate, coffee liqueur and rum. A creamy rum and vanilla mixture is marbled into a dark chocolate, coffee and liqueur mixture, poured into an amaretti biscuit shell and baked. The torte is then cooled and chilled thoroughly before serving.

SERVES 8-10

BISCUIT CASE
275 g (10 oz) amaretti
    biscuits, ratafias or
    macaroons
125 g (4 oz) unsalted butter
FILLING
700 g (1½ lb) mascarpone
    or Philadelphia cream
    cheese (at room
    temperature)
150 g (5 oz) caster sugar
3 eggs, separated
30 g (1 oz) plain flour
45 ml (3 tbsp) dark rum
2.5 ml (½ tsp) vanilla
    essence
175 g (6 oz) plain dark
    chocolate
15 ml (1 tbsp) finely ground
    espresso coffee
45 ml (3 tbsp) Tia Maria or
    other coffee liqueur
TO FINISH
icing sugar, for dusting
    (optional)

PREPARATION TIME
40 minutes, plus chilling
COOKING TIME
45 minutes
FREEZING
Suitable

910-735 CALS PER SERVING

1. Place the biscuits in a blender or food processor and process until finely ground. Melt 75 g (3 oz) unsalted butter and stir in the crumbs until well coated. Spoon into a 23 cm (9 inch) loose-bottomed springform cake tin. Press evenly over the base and 4 cm (1½ inches) up the sides with the back of a spoon to form a neat shell. Chill for at least 30 minutes until firm.

2. Preheat the oven to 200°C (400°F) Mark 6. Using a wooden spoon or in an electric mixer, beat the cream cheese until smooth. Add the sugar and beat again until smooth, then beat in the egg yolks. Divide the mixture in half and stir the flour, rum and vanilla into one half.

3. Melt the chocolate in a bowl over a pan of simmering water, cool slightly, then stir in the coffee and coffee liqueur. Stir into the remaining half of the cheese mixture. Whisk the egg whites until just holding soft peaks and fold half into each flavoured cheese mixture.

4. Quickly spoon alternate mounds of the two cheese mixtures into the set biscuit case until full. Using a knife, swirl the mixtures together to produce a marbled effect.

5. Bake in the oven for 45 minutes, covering the top with foil if it appears to be over-browning. At this stage the torte

will be soft in the middle. Leave in the switched-off oven with the door slightly ajar, to cool completely; it will continue to firm up during this time. Chill for several hours before serving, to allow the flavours to develop.

6. If preferred, dust the top of the cheesecake with icing sugar. Serve cut into wedges, with crème fraîche if desired.

NOTE: Use a potato masher to press the crumbs evenly over the base of the loose-bottomed cake tin.

VARIATION

Substitute an equal quantity of chocolate digestives for the amaretti biscuits and proceed in the same way.

TECHNIQUE

Using the end of a sharp knife, swirl the two different flavoured cheese mixtures together to produce a marbled pattern.

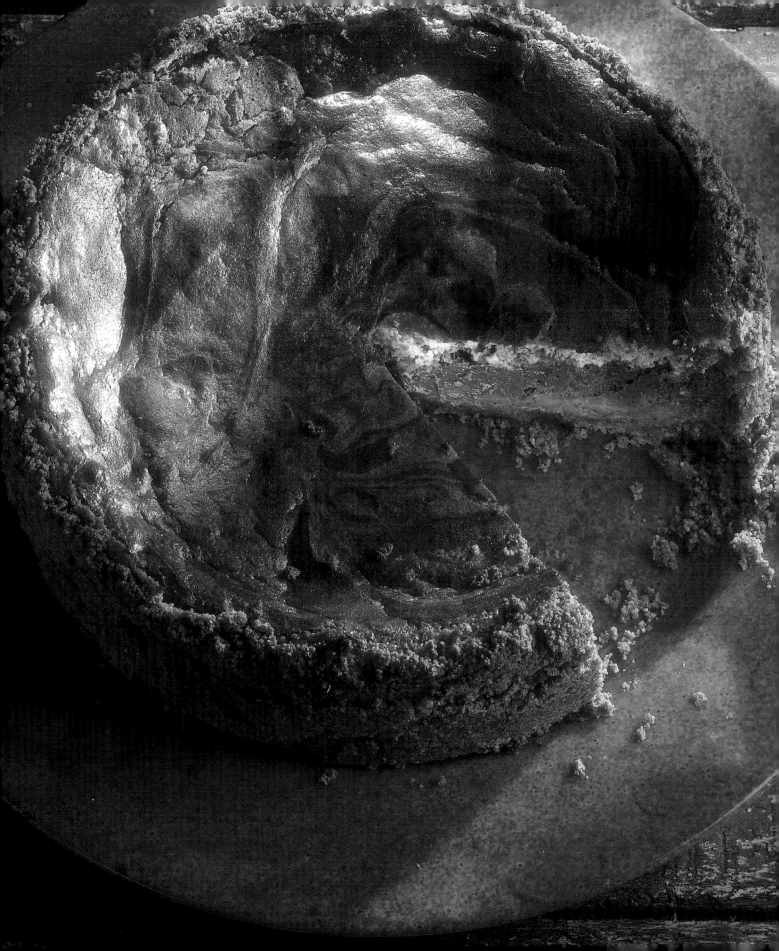

WALNUT TART WITH CARAMEL ICE CREAM

Walnuts and caramel are a marriage made in heaven! Walnuts are encased in an irresistible gooey fudge mixture in this tart. The accompanying soft caramel ice cream is easy to make and does not require stirring during freezing. Watch that the caramel doesn't become too dark or the ice cream will be bitter.

SERVES 8-10

CARAMEL ICE CREAM
225 g (8 oz) granulated
   sugar
300 ml (½ pint) milk
300 ml (½ pint) double
   cream
8 egg yolks
PASTRY
225 g (8 oz) plain white flour
30 ml (2 tbsp) icing sugar
125 g (4 oz) butter
2 egg yolks
FILLING
125 g (4 oz) unsalted butter,
   softened
125 g (4 oz) light soft brown
   sugar
3 eggs
finely grated rind and juice
   of 1 small orange
175 g (6 oz) golden syrup
225 g (8 oz) shelled walnut
   pieces
pinch of salt

PREPARATION TIME
1 hour, plus freezing
COOKING TIME
1 hour
FREEZING
Suitable

1065-850 CALS PER SERVING

1. To make the ice cream, put the sugar in a saucepan with 150 ml (¼ pint) water. Dissolve over a low heat until clear. Increase the heat and boil rapidly until the sugar begins to caramelise.

2. Remove from the heat and leave the caramel to stand for 2-3 minutes; it will turn a deep amber brown colour. Pour on the milk and cream, stirring (see technique); then whisk in the egg yolks. Return to a gentle heat and stir, without letting the custard boil, for about 15 minutes until slightly thickened. Allow to cool, then chill.

3. Freeze the ice cream, using an ice cream machine if you have one. Alternatively, pour the mixture into a freezer-proof container and freeze until firm.

4. To make the pastry, sift the flour and icing sugar together into a bowl and rub in the butter. Stir in the egg yolks and enough iced water to bind to a firm dough. Knead lightly until smooth. Wrap in cling film and chill for 30 minutes.

5. Preheat the oven to 200°C (400°F) Mark 6. Roll out the pastry thinly and use to line a 23 cm (9 inch) fluted flan tin. Chill for 20 minutes. Line with greaseproof paper and baking beans and bake blind for 15-20 minutes, removing

the paper and beans for the last 5 minutes. Reduce the oven setting to 180°C (350°F) Mark 4.

6. To make the filling, cream the butter and sugar together until light and fluffy. Gradually beat in the eggs, one at a time, then stir in the orange rind and juice. Heat the syrup until runny, but not very hot, then stir into the filling with the walnuts and salt. Pour into the flan case and bake for 40-45 minutes until lightly browned and risen. (The tart will sink a little on cooling.) Serve warm or cold, in slices with a scoop of caramel ice cream.

NOTE: The ice cream will always be a little soft owing to the high quantity of sugar. Serve straight from the freezer.

TECHNIQUE

Carefully pour the milk and cream onto the caramel, stirring. The mixture almost sets at this stage, but dissolves on heating.

TWO-CHOCOLATE LACE PANCAKES

Dark, chocolate-flavoured lacy pancakes are filled with a rich white chocolate mousse, then served dusted with cocoa and icing sugar on a lake of single cream. You will find that a little of the filling goes a long way. Try rolling and folding the pancakes in different ways.

SERVES 6

PANCAKES
125 g (4 oz) plain white
    flour, less 30 ml (2 tbsp)
30 ml (2 tbsp) cocoa powder
15 ml (1 tbsp) icing sugar
pinch of salt
1 egg, plus 1 egg yolk
300 ml (½ pint) milk
15 ml (1 tbsp) sunflower oil
a little extra oil, for cooking
CHOCOLATE MOUSSE
250 g (9 oz) quality white
    chocolate (see note)
30 ml (2 tbsp) Grand
    Marnier or other orange-
    flavoured liqueur
350 ml (12 fl oz) double
    cream
TO SERVE
150 ml (¼ pint) single
    cream
cocoa powder, for dusting
icing sugar, for dusting

PREPARATION TIME
45 minutes, plus chilling
COOKING TIME
2 minutes per pancake
FREEZING
Suitable: Pancakes only
(interleaved with greaseproof)

715 CALS PER SERVING

1. Place all the ingredients for the pancakes in a blender or food processor and work until smooth. Pour into a jug and leave to rest in a cool place for at least 30 minutes.

2. Heat a 15 cm (6 inch) crêpe pan until very hot and wipe with a little oil. (The hotter the pan the lacier your crêpes will be). Pour in about 30 ml (2 tbsp) batter, quickly swirling it around the pan. Don't worry if there are small holes in the pancake – they will look good in the final version! As soon as it sets, turn over and cook the other side. Transfer to a warmed plate and continue until all the batter is used up, heating the pan well each time and interleaving the cooked pancakes with greaseproof paper to prevent them sticking. You should have sufficient batter for 12 pancakes.

3. To make the mousse, chop the chocolate into tiny pieces and place in a heatproof bowl with the liqueur and 45 ml (3 tbsp) water. Stand over a pan of hot water and stir constantly until the chocolate is melted and smooth. Allow to cool until tepid.

4. Whisk the cream until it forms soft peaks and fold into the chocolate mixture. Working quickly – as the mousse sets fast – place 30 ml (2 tbsp) on each

pancake and roll or fold carefully to enclose the filling. Place on a tray as you go. Chill for at least 1 hour.

5. To serve, pour a little single cream onto each serving plate and place two pancakes on top. Dust liberally with cocoa powder, then icing sugar. Serve immediately.

NOTE: Use only white chocolate that has been made with pure cocoa butter for optimum flavour and texture. Lindt and Tobler are both suitable brands. The pancakes should look delicate when filled – don't make them too large!

TECHNIQUE

Fold each lacy pancake around 30 ml (2 tbsp) of the mousse filling, working as quickly as possible.

COCONUT BAVAROIS WITH TROPICAL FRUIT SAUCE

A pretty pale creamy moulded custard, flecked with little specks of vanilla, cloaked and floating on a golden sea of mango and passion fruit sauce. The truly tropical tastes of coconut, mango and passion fruit are given a lift by using coconut liqueur and orange and lime juice.

SERVES 6

400 ml (14 fl oz) can
   coconut milk
1 vanilla pod
200 ml (7 fl oz) milk
4 egg yolks
125 g (4 oz) caster sugar
25 ml (5 tsp) powdered
   gelatine
30-45 ml (2-3 tbsp) coconut
   liqueur
150 ml (¼ pint) double
   cream

FRUIT SAUCE

1 large ripe mango, about
   450 g (1 lb)
juice of 1 large orange
juice of 1 lime
2 ripe wrinkly passion fruit
icing sugar, to taste

TO DECORATE

mint sprigs
finely shredded orange and
   lime rinds (optional)

PREPARATION TIME
30 minutes, plus chilling
COOKING TIME
15-20 minutes
FREEZING
Suitable: Sauce only

500 CALS PER SERVING

1. Pour the coconut milk into a non-aluminium saucepan and whisk well to mix. Split the vanilla pod lengthways and scrape the black seeds into the coconut milk. Stir in the milk, heat to boiling point, then remove from the heat.

2. Whisk the egg yolks and sugar together until pale and fluffy. Pour on the coconut milk and stir well. Return to the pan and cook over a gentle heat, stirring all the time, for about 15 minutes until slightly thickened to the consistency of double cream; do not boil or it will curdle. Strain into a bowl, cover the surface with damp greaseproof paper to prevent a skin forming, and allow to cool.

3. Put 50 ml (2 fl oz) cold water in a small bowl and sprinkle on the gelatine. Leave until softened and sponge-like, then stand the bowl in a pan of simmering water and stir occasionally until dissolved. Stir thoroughly into the cold custard with the coconut liqueur. Chill for 15-20 minutes until the custard begins to thicken; check and stir every 5 minutes.

4. Lightly oil six 150 ml (¼ pint) individual moulds. Whip cream until holding soft peaks, then fold into the custard. Carefully spoon into the moulds and tap each one on the work surface to knock out large air bubbles. Cover and chill for at least 2-3 hours until set.

5. To make the sauce, peel the mango and cut the flesh away from the stone. Place in a blender or food processor with the orange and lime juices. Purée until smooth, then pass through a sieve into a bowl. Halve the passion fruit and scoop out the seeds into the mango sauce. Stir in icing sugar to taste. If the sauce is a little thick, thin with a little more orange juice. Chill.

6. To serve, run a thin-bladed knife around each bavarois and invert onto a dessert plate. Spoon over a little of the sauce and pour the rest around the bavarois. Decorate with mint and shreds of orange and lime rinds, if desired.

TECHNIQUE

Halve the passion fruit and scoop out the seeds and pulp into the mango sauce.

PISTACHIO PRALINE FLOATING ISLANDS

Soft pillows of poached meringue speckled with green and amber pieces of pistachio praline – floating on a lake of delicate pale yellow custard – makes an impressive dessert. The praline can, of course, be made well ahead and stored in an airtight container until required.

SERVES 4-6

PRALINE
50 g (2 oz) unskinned pistachio nuts
50 g (2 oz) caster sugar
FLOATING ISLANDS
2 eggs, separated
150 g (5 oz) caster sugar
300 ml (½ pint) single cream
300 ml (½ pint) milk

PREPARATION TIME
30 minutes, plus chilling
COOKING TIME
18-20 minutes
FREEZING
Not suitable

520-350 CALS PER SERVING

1. First make the praline. Lightly oil a baking sheet. Put the pistachios and sugar in a small heavy-based saucepan over a gentle heat and stir with a metal spoon until the sugar melts and begins to caramelise. Continue to cook until the mixture is a deep brown colour, then immediately pour onto the oiled baking sheet. Leave to cool completely, then pound to a coarse powder in a food processor or blender.

2. To make the meringue, whisk the egg whites in a bowl until they form soft peaks. Gradually whisk in 75 g (3 oz) of the caster sugar until the mixture is very stiff and shiny. Quickly and carefully fold in all but 30 ml (2 tbsp) of the praline.

3. Place the cream, milk and remaining sugar in a medium saucepan and bring to a gentle simmer. Spoon 5-6 small rounds of meringue mixture into the pan and cook gently for 2-3 minutes, or until they have doubled in size and are quite firm to the touch. Remove with a slotted spoon and drain on kitchen paper. Repeat with the remaining mixture: you should have 12-18 meringues, depending on size.

4. Whisk the egg yolks into the poaching liquid. Heat gently, stirring all the time, until the custard thickens slightly to the consistency of double cream; do not allow to boil or it will curdle.

5. Strain the custard into a serving dish, or individual dishes, and position the meringues on top. Cool, then chill for 30 minutes. Serve sprinkled with the remaining praline.

NOTE: The meringues can be made a few hours in advance and kept floating on the custard. Sprinkle with praline just before serving.

VARIATIONS

Use hazelnuts or almonds instead of the pistachios. Add a pinch of cinnamon or nutmeg to the custard.

TECHNIQUE

As soon as the caramel and nut mixture turns a deep brown colour, carefully pour it onto the oiled baking sheet.

BROWN SUGAR MERINGUES WITH RASPBERRY SAUCE

Generous clouds of meringue are filled with whipped cream and sliced peaches and served on a sharp ruby red sauce. Demerara sugar adds a slight caramel flavour to the meringues and colours them a pretty, pale beige. Use nectarines instead of peaches, or strawberries, if you prefer.

SERVES 6

MERINGUE
4 egg whites
125 g (4 oz) granulated sugar
125 g (4 oz) demerara sugar
RASPBERRY SAUCE
450 g (1 lb) fresh or frozen raspberries, thawed
30 ml (2 tbsp) lemon juice
icing sugar, to taste
30 ml (2 tbsp) kirsch
TO ASSEMBLE
2-3 ripe peaches
15 ml (1 tbsp) kirsch
300 ml (½ pint) double cream

PREPARATION TIME
35 minutes, plus cooling
COOKING TIME
3-4 hours
FREEZING
Not suitable

375 CALS PER SERVING

1. Preheat the oven to 110°C (225 °F) Mark ¼. Put the egg whites in a large bowl and whisk until very stiff but not dry. Gradually whisk in the combined sugars, spoonful by spoonful, allowing the mixture to become very stiff between each addition.

2. Line a baking sheet with non-stick baking parchment. Spoon or pipe about 12 meringues onto the parchment. Bake in the oven for 3-4 hours until thoroughly dried out.

3. Remove the meringues from the oven and leave to cool on the parchment. Carefully lift off when cool and store in an airtight container until required.

4. To make the raspberry sauce, place the raspberries in a blender or food processor with the lemon juice and icing sugar to taste. Work to a purée, then pass through a sieve to remove any seeds. Stir in the kirsch, cover and chill in the refrigerator.

5. Immerse the peaches in a bowl of boiling water for 20 seconds to loosen the skins. Lift out and plunge into cold water to stop further cooking. Peel off the skins. Halve the peaches and remove the stones. Slice neatly and sprinkle with 15 ml (1 tbsp) kirsch.

6. To serve, whip the cream until it just holds soft peaks. Spoon the cream onto six of the meringues. Arrange the sliced peaches on top and sandwich together with the remaining meringues. Place on individual serving plates and pour over the raspberry sauce. Serve immediately.

NOTE: The secret to making these meringues is to whisk the egg whites initially until very stiff and to whisk until stiff between each addition of sugar. Do not add the sugar too quickly, or the meringue will become thin.

TECHNIQUE

Shape the meringue into large ovals, using two tablespoons and place on a baking sheet lined with non-stick baking parchment.

RHUBARB AND GINGER ICE CREAM

Rhubarb and ginger are a favourite combination in my native Scotland where everyone's grandmother makes the best rhubarb and ginger jam! The ice cream can be pale pink or green depending on the type of rhubarb – adding a drop of natural food colouring enhances the colour. Dainty ginger biscuits are the perfect complement.

SERVES 4

350 g (12 oz) trimmed rhubarb stalks

50 g (2 oz) sugar, or to taste

75 g (3 oz) stem ginger in syrup, drained and syrup reserved

150 ml (¼ pint) single cream

150 ml (¼ pint) double cream

2 egg yolks

GINGER BISCUITS

50 g (2 oz) butter

25 g (1 oz) caster sugar

75 g (3 oz) plain white flour

5 ml (1 tsp) ground ginger

extra caster sugar, for dusting

TO DECORATE

a little chopped stem ginger in syrup, drained

PREPARATION TIME
45 minutes, plus freezing
COOKING TIME
40 minutes
FREEZING
Suitable: Ice cream only

495 CALS PER SERVING

1. Cut the rhubarb into chunks and place in a saucepan with the sugar and 30 ml (2 tbsp) ginger syrup. Cover, bring to the boil, lower the heat and simmer for 15-20 minutes until very tender. Allow to cool slightly, then purée in a blender or food processor until smooth. Cool. Chop the ginger finely and add to the rhubarb purée. Chill.

2. Pour the two creams into a saucepan and bring to the boil. Whisk the egg yolks together in a bowl, then whisk in the scalded creams. Return to the pan. Stir the custard over a very gentle heat for about 15 minutes until thickened to the consistency of double cream. Remove from the heat, cover the surface with greaseproof paper to prevent a skin forming and allow to cool, then chill.

3. Stir the custard into the chilled rhubarb mixture, then taste and add more ginger syrup if necessary. Freeze in an ice cream machine, according to the manufacturer's directions. Alternatively, turn into a freezerproof container, cover and freeze until firm, whisking occasionally (see note).

4. To make the ginger biscuits, cream the butter and sugar together in a bowl. Sift the flour and ginger together over the mixture, then beat in thoroughly.

When the mixture forms a ball, knead lightly, then roll out on a floured surface to a 3 mm (⅛ inch) thickness. Using a biscuit cutter, cut out shapes and place on a baking sheet. Chill for 15 minutes.

5. Preheat the oven to 190°C (375°F) Mark 5, then bake the biscuits for 10-15 minutes. Sprinkle with caster sugar whilst still warm. Leave to cool.

6. Scoop the ice cream into serving dishes and top with a little chopped ginger. Serve with the ginger biscuits.

NOTE: If you are not using an ice cream maker it is important to whisk the mixture periodically during freezing to break down the ice crystals and ensure a smooth-textured result.

TECHNIQUE

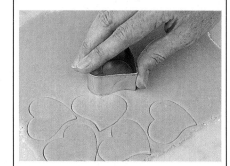

Using a small heart-shaped or round cutter, stamp out the biscuits.

If you would like further information about the **Good Housekeeping Cookery Club**, please write to:
Penny Smith, Ebury Press, Random House, 20 Vauxhall Bridge Road, London SW1V 2SA.